500 CEOs:
Lessons From The Heart

Gordon F. Holbein

500 CEOs:
Lessons From The Heart

ISBN-13: 978-1534685062
ISBN-10: 1534685065

OVERVIEW

How would you like to chat with over 500 intelligent, experienced and successful leaders working in dozens of industries on four continents around the world? What would you ask them? Would you like to hear their real life stories, how they earned their victories and how they coped with their mistakes and failures?

Picture yourself meeting one-on-one with the top executive of a company of interest to you. They greet you warmly, and inquire about your life, your interests, and how they can assist you. You appreciate their generosity of time and spirit, and perceive how genuine and down-to-earth they are. They ask, "How may I help you? What do you need to know?"

This book is the product of more than seven-hundred interviews conducted over a period of almost fifteen years. The concluding question in each interview was: "What advice do you have for those who are early in their careers?"

Without exception, these experienced and successful leaders opened their hearts, and shared key insights on practical topics such career development, leadership, problem-solving and decision-making, communication skills, networking, education and learning. And yet the most heartfelt and evocative messages came in their discussions of topics such as passion, ethics and integrity, humility, risk-taking, mistakes and failure, touch and intuition.

Not surprisingly, not all our leaders agree on every topic. Their varied perspectives are intriguing and enlightening. Those views which differ from yours are where you will discover your greatest opportunities for learning and growth.

Many of the comments here cover multiple topics in one response so chapter "boundaries" are a bit fuzzy. What you find in one chapter may apply well to others too. When you find similar advice repeated, consider why some things bear reinforcing multiple times.

Clearly, not all the lessons in here pertain to you now. But they likely will at a later stage in your growth.

These lessons are for people in all walks of life. Whether you work in the corporate world, or simply want to reflect on great ideas, wander through these observations, bits of advice, and challenges slowly. Take in a thought at a time. Apply the keys you discover in your daily work and life. Then share your growth with others.

Background Facts

Of the 700-plus interviews recorded through the years, 540 are included here. There are 980 quotations presented in these pages. The numbers you see by each quotation may help you discover multiple quotations from the same CEOs.

Approximately 4% of our CEOs were women. While more than 90% of the 700-plus interviews were with CEOs based in the United States, other nations represented are: Brazil, Canada, China, England, France, Germany, India, Ireland, Japan, Mexico, Singapore, and South Korea.

This table presents the distribution of corporations represented across various economic sectors.

Sector	Count	Percent
Manufacturing	89	16%
Financial Services	71	13%
Healthcare	51	9%
Consumer Products	45	8%
Business Services	36	7%
Energy, Mining & Materials	35	6%
Retailing	34	6%
Entertainment & Media	28	5%
Information Technology	25	5%
Agriculture	23	4%
Construction	22	4%
Hospitality	22	4%
Consumer Services	16	3%
Utilities	13	2%
Transportation	12	2%
Conglomerates	9	2%
Real Estate	5	1%
Biotechnology	4	1%

ACKNOWLEDGEMENTS

During the past 25 years, I have had the wonderful privilege and pleasure of working with more than 2,500 students in my undergraduate and MBA courses in Strategic Management. These interactions have evolved with time. And as I have become more experienced, I am increasingly humbled by what I learn from them. They have consistently opened my eyes and my mind.

Four students who provided extraordinary conceptual and practical support for this project from its earliest days deserve special recognition and appreciation: Adam Lucas, Ben Smith, Haley Prevatt, and Nick Minneman. Many sincere thanks to all.

TABLE OF CONTENTS

ART AND SCIENCE

Science is about knowing. It involves rules, objectivity, measurement, replication, techniques, control. Art is about interpreting. It involves sense, subjectivity, intuitiveness, creativity, challenging convention, playfulness. In this way, much of what we do is a little bit science and a lot of art. It is a craft.

44. "Management is more art than science. You must have a dream or a vision, build a plan, and build a team to make it happen, but be ready to 'redraw the picture' as the customer, the business, or the industry changes. In your classes, you learn a lot about the 'science,' but don't forget the art. (Ms. S. – Retailing)

48. "Strategic management is a science-based art. You can go to college for six or seven years learning the science behind management, but that does not mean you are going to apply it right. You need a certain touch to understand the environment in which we live. Managing strategically is all about the art of connecting the right dots at the right times." (Mr. M. – Healthcare)

74. "Every MBA should endeavor to develop the art of strategic management which can only be done through experience. Many MBAs are well versed in the science of management, but one can only develop their own unique style through the experience of working with and managing others. This is the most important thing that I look for when hiring for key positions in the company." (Mr. D. – Healthcare)

83.   "Strategic management is an art, not a science. You need to understand that strategy is a clear result of a messy process. It is true that some strategy is formed in planning meetings, but strategy is determined just as much by informal conversations in the hallway and in meetings on topics other than strategy. In sum, strategy is a messy process and cannot be defined in a textbook fashion." (Mr. D. – Retailing)

148.   "Look at the art and science of strategic management. Students should be taught to see trends on the science side and marry that with the gut or art so that you are there when it happens. By 'there' I mean able to take advantage of a trend." (Mr. L. – Entertainment & Media)

201.   "New MBAs need to understand that effective strategic management has two parts: analysis and synthesis. In MBA coursework students get a good foundation for the analysis part, but struggle with the synthesis part. In management positions, many new MBAs get caught up in the analysis of the data – paralysis by analysis – and therefore miss the synthesis part. I see this to be true whether it is formulation or implementation. MBAs need to develop an instinct for the situation and the meaning of the data." (Mr. M. – Business Services)

204.   "Managing strategically is both a science and an art. On the science side, formulating strategies is necessarily formulaic. You can't plug and play, but it's about cobbling together pieces from different areas. This allows you to have a defined focus, to set your mission and goals, and to measure metrics. On the art side it's about working through problems. This may

include intuition and creativity to see what hasn't been seen." (Mr. M. – Information Technology)

271. "Most business school graduates expect management to be a science, however in business two and two doesn't necessarily equal four." (Mr. G. – Retailing)

319. "I must emphasize the idea of blending art and science together. I feel as though both are crucial elements in leadership, strategy and management. The science aspect can be used to find which tools and approaches are of value. The art side will facilitate these tools. With art and science together, you can leverage everything in practice." (Mr. W. – Transportation)

323. "A scene that I would like to use to explain a role of a strategic manager comes from the movie U-571. Bill Paxton plays a submarine captain during the World War II. At one point he tries to explain to Matthew McConaughey what it takes to be a submarine captain. Paxton says, 'As a captain you cannot hesitate; you have to act. If you don't, you put the entire crew at risk. That's the job. It is not a science. You have to make decisions based on imperfect information, asking men to follow orders that may result in their death, and if you are wrong you suffer the consequences. If you can't do this, then you've got no reason to be a captain.'" (Mr. J. – Construction)

427. "Strategic management is part science, and a lot art. It is very fluid, and calls for the ability to change as needed because there are lots of theories out there, a new hot topic every year or so." (Ms. S. – Retailing)

434.   "Never forget that managing an organization is part art and part science. Spend your time in school learning the science. The only way you will learn the art is the experience of doing it over time." (Mr. H. – Hospitality)

450.   "With strategic management you have tactical components, but learning the art of management is learning to read people. As manager you've got to read people. You've got to understand whether they are stressed about their job, whether they have issues at home, whether they want your job, whether they aspire to other things, etc. You've got to be able to read all that on a daily basis." (Ms. B. – Food & Food & Agriculture)

511.   "I think the role of a CEO is a function of both art and science. But it can't become an art without the foundation of science. Its going to be important, especially in this day and age, to have a knowledge and understanding of the position you hold – that's the science. But how you use this information to better the company as a whole is what distinguishes you – that's the art. You have to have that educational base though. How you use the knowledge you've accumulated toward the betterment of the company is what sets people apart." (Mr. M. – Entertainment & Media)

527.   "People coming out of college think that they have all the answers. And yes, you have gotten really book smart, but from a business world standpoint it is an art not a science, like I said earlier. You have got to be open minded, continually willing to learn; if you do those things, they can be beneficial for you." (Mr. J. – Manufacturing)

572. "The process of how you apply your decisions is a science. But the art is just your gut feeling. That's where you have to rely on the people directly below you. You know, I can't see everything; that's the art we're talking about. I mean, things change so much it's impossible to account for all those variables." (Mr. S. – Utilities)

653. "Strategic management is more a state of mind, a spirit, it's a large window. Reality is not rational, it is emotional." (Mr. L. – Information Technology)

BUSINESS OPERATIONS

Many executives, when describing how and why they have made strategic decisions, use the wording: "We feel that…" Note that in order to "feel" the sense of a situation, one must be in touch with what is actually going on. One must be close to the action in order to feel right about their decisions. Also, note the word "we." Truly strategic leaders do not act from a position of remote isolation. They connect with those who are doing the actual work. So, we must get beyond our theories, and beyond our narrow disciplines. We must know our business personally, intimately, and fully.

29.   "It is so important to not only know what you want, but how to get it as well. Just because you have a great idea; it doesn't necessarily mean that it is a workable idea. Many MBA students are great thinkers, but they need to understand that their ideas aren't usable if they aren't workable in the company. An MBA student's ideas need to go hand-in-hand with the business; therefore they need to be able to understand the business model because it is crucial in running a business." (Mr. D. – Energy, Mining & Materials)

30.   "Refine your understanding of the business. Develop insight into the business. Understand the industry." (Mr. A. – Financial Services)

38.   "Take some time when you are initially hired to learn how the company really works. Pay less

attention to the strategic plan and staffing charts, and pay more attention to the subtleties of the company's operation. Once you understand the company's core operations and processes, then you can help in the company's strategic management." (Mr. C. – Business Services)

77. "As a person entering a new field or job, it is important to understand that a successful employee is patient. He or she is not going to catapult their way to the top without learning from the bottom up. Do not be ashamed to learn the technical side of an industry before attempting to move towards the strategy." (Mr. R. – Financial Services)

88. "The most important concept to understand about strategic management is that the successful executive should identify where the business makes most of its revenues and take an active role in that activity. For example, what functions, plants, product lines, etc. drive most of the revenues? If you are not engaged in this, you are on the fringe of success at best." (Dr. D. – Business Services)

100. "What seems to be lacking in young professionals is some real world exposure in operations. Not having operational experience is a problem because without it you cannot know what the possibilities are. An analogy is planning a road trip. Look at the road to success as just that – a road trip. Look at any map and see how many routes there are to a destination. Keep this in mind on your journey because one roadblock does not mean the ride is over. It just means it's time to pull out the map and pick a different route." (Mr. P. – Retailing)

110.   "Get a line job, which is where you get most of your knowledge, as class studies will not teach you everything, and staff positions generally do not lead to the top." (Mr. M. – Manufacturing)

139.   "You need to realize that you can't concentrate on simply being strategic thinkers. There is more to life and more to management than that. The purpose of management – as with any support position – is to make things run more effectively and efficiently. So you have to ask yourself on a daily basis, 'Am I achieving that objective?' You need to be close to the product because ultimately that's why you have your job – to ensure that the product is created and sold, and that the company turns a profit at the end of the day. It seems simple, but it's frankly not. It's complicated and fraught with risk." (Mr. C. – Energy, Mining & Materials)

140.   "Never stop learning.   Immerse yourself in every aspect of the business.   The more you know about your company, the better you can understand how things actually work, and the better you can make decisions about it." (Mr. W. – Real Estate)

148.   "Even if you have a great personality and great communication skills, but are not able to monitor and control the business, you have compromised your ability to contribute." (Mr. L. – Entertainment & Media)

170.   "Value creation is critical in any business. That value creation determines your competitive advantage. Long-term value creation leads to sustainable advantage. Concentrate on your most valuable customers, the ones your profit is most dependent on,

and avoid being sidetracked." (Mr. K. – Information Technology)

180. "You need practical experience. Go to work after college, and work for a few years; then maybe get an MBA. Operational knowledge is key in order to get things done. Many can talk strategy, but can't get the job done. Many people I've met knew strategy, but failed on operational implementation. It is hard to do operations, but easy to strategize. In order to understand strategy, you have to live and understand the real workings of your business. Operationally, going from location 1 to 2 can be more difficult than developing the strategy itself. People need to learn the financial part of the business, and one still needs to know about operations." (Mr. O. – Manufacturing)

190. "First, one cannot be a totally 'strategic' manager. This is especially true for small to mid-sized companies. A manager must get in the trenches and pull levers to make a company work. One must put in time and gain experience because strategies do not work without an understanding and knowledge of the firm's actual operations." (Mr. D. – Biotechnology)

214. "Start out from a low level position, especially if you have experience in sales, customer services, or operations management. It is important to be fully involved in the business and feel the business and learn how the business works. Low level experience serves as good practice for what you learned from your classes. Also, you can learn something new that is difficult to understand without personal involvement in the specific situation. Most MBA students learn the business very fast due to their excellent educational

background. When you go up to higher management levels, you will be very confident dealing with complex problems and challenges. The opportunity to succeed in higher management positions is much higher for those MBA students with extensive ground floor experience. I see lots of MBA students fail in upper management because they are without low level experience. Also, you can afford to make some mistakes in low level jobs. But you cannot afford such mistakes in the higher level positions." (Mr. P. – Manufacturing)

223.   "Students must really understand the business inside and out to be able to develop a successful strategy." (Mr. H. – Hospitality)

231.   "Get to know your company, your industry, and your customers very well. This will help you to be able to persuade them to follow what you believe and go in the same direction as the business." (Mr. H. – Consumer Products)

248.   "Take on all new challenges and opportunities. Work in all new areas so you can understand how each department supports each other." (Mr. G. – Utilities)

284.   "The best thing you can do early in your career is get as much exposure to as much of the functionality as you can. Then you are getting the business view. If you get yourself too far into the engineering side, or too far into the accounting side, the risk is that in a large corporation you get stuck there because you don't have the ability to have interaction." (Mr. R. – Manufacturing)

291. "You must understand what your boss or upper management wants from the staff and what they are looking for exactly so there is clear communication. One will begin to understand how they make decisions or see things in their perspective. From my own experience, most upper management in operations or manufacturing will need the facts interpreted through numbers and figures. This part of manufacturing is usually done by the Controller of the plant, or someone in the accounting area. If someone in manufacturing could understand the financial aspect of what the actions on the shop floor mean, and could interpret those figures from operations to financials and back to operations, they could be a great asset to a company. So learn the operational and financial side of things, how they tie together, and how to explain them back and forth. Learn how to tie the different areas of a company together to interpret them to other areas of the business. This is a big reason why companies have rotations with their younger business professionals. There is a great advantage for someone who works in the different areas of the business, especially when they start to manage their own part of the business. The biggest problem that people have is doing these things repetitively." (Mr. B. – Manufacturing)

294. "Regardless of how many letters are behind someone's name, experience and learning a company from the ground up is an irreplaceable and necessary trait." (Mr. M. – Manufacturing)

304. "You have to get real world exposure, not the exposure that shows how good the business world can be. Things like role shadowing only show one side of

the experience. They never show you the experiences of being there when times are tough. Experience is learning how to act and work when there is a 'fire.'" (Mr. S. – Construction)

329. "Strong execution and implementation are as important as creative ideas and so-called strategic thinking." (Mr. B. – Retailing)

342. "Strategic management is mostly execution. You must get the job done. Strategy can be very simple, in fact our business is not complex at all. But you must stay focused to be an effective strategic manager and want to get it done." (Mr. H. – Consumer Products)

343. "Seek to understand your company and its environment before you attempt to change it. Perhaps through years of experience there is a reason that things have landed they way they have. The advice you want to bring to the table may have already been tried, tested, failed and adapted to the processes that exist now. Unless you make the attempt to understand your surroundings, you will never know this and ultimately waste time trying the same things that have already failed." (Mr. M. – Healthcare)

355. "Understand that you do not really see the big picture until you get out into it. You can theorize and do simulations all you want, but you will not truly understand the business world until you get into it. So do not be taken by surprise." (Mr. K. – Energy, Mining & Materials)

356. "It is very important to realize that entities that have a well-defined strategic theory are not always

successful. I have witnessed failed companies so involved with developing a vision or mission statement and strategic formulation, when they should have been concerned with successful execution." (Mr. S. – Energy, Mining & Materials)

371.   "You need to get around business; you can only learn so much in a classroom. If you were to start working with us, what you'd learn in the first 30 days would probably equal what you've learned in the past year and a half of school. Coming in, you'd say, 'Oh, this is how this really works.' And have some financial sense to yourself. Accounting – I kick myself daily – I learned it and had some classes, but I wish I had known more about accounting – the general ledger, balance sheet, and all that stuff." (Mr. K. – Consumer Products)

374.   "All strategic management initiatives need to be weighed against practical real life situations." (Mr. G. – Business Services)

375.   "You must realize that you're going to have to pay your dues to get trust and respect in a company. Those promoting you – eventually the Board of Directors – have to know and be comfortable with you, and believe that you have the knowledge and ability that are needed to lead. They have to have the realization that you know what you are talking about, that you've done it, and that you understand how to operate the business. So there is just no substitution for spending time in the trenches." (Mr. H. – Manufacturing)

388.   "You have to learn from the ground up, acquire technical skills, and observe and figure out what it is

that makes a company successful. Leverage is based upon experience and careful thought, not just something you learn in a book. You have to be able to understand the inner workings of a company in great detail, and that takes experience in addition to a good education." (Mr. F. – Financial Services)

408. "Execution is in many cases a lost art. There are tons of people out there that have great ideas. Execution is the real variable that makes the difference because there are a lot of people that have great ideas, but they can't execute. There are a lot of people that have okay ideas, but can they execute? When you can execute, that's all the difference in the world. That's what makes it work. Execution isn't sexy – it's not exciting – but that's what makes things work, and I think that is as important as the strategy." (Mr. T. – Financial Services)

423. "Do the dirty work no matter what it pays. Learn the details and be willing to take risks. Don't think those little tasks don't lead to something because they all lead to something." (Mr. H. – Consumer Services)

447. "In order to be an excellent CEO, you must understand everything that is involved in operating a company including accounting, operations, sales, and information technology. Put the time in." (Mr. S. – Healthcare)

452. "The more you can learn about all facets of an organization, the better off you are. It will give you more potential there and at other organizations. Our previous CEO really took the time to involve me in

every part of our organization which is what allowed me to take over when he retired." (Ms. A. – Biotechnology)

453. "I think having a rock solid background in accounting, financial management, corporate tax laws, and industry regulations is certainly critical. And if you can couple that with a practical and meaningful way of coordinating all the elements of business by being able to relate to all factions associated with the business – from the rank and file line employees to government officials – then you'll be on the track to success. Keeping up with IT and understanding the technical side of things through continuing education is something you have to fully embrace in order to remain competitive and successful." (Mr. A. – Manufacturing)

467. "You need to know the business, the customers, the human resources, and have studied the markets. I think that's really important from a strategic standpoint. Know your markets, your demand, your future projections. You have to watch for those things. You have got to see if your markets are going to be changing, or if you'll have to provide something that you haven't provided before, and plan on those too. And I think that's probably the hardest part of it." (Mr. S. – Energy, Mining & Materials)

470. "Just one or two things. One is, wherever you work figure out what makes the place tick. Figure out what it is it's trying to do, what its product is. It doesn't have to be a tangible 'product.' It could be an intellectual product. It could be many things, but figure it out. It could be a college or university. How do you

measure if it's successful? Figure that out and focus on it. And then figure out who within that organization are the key people; those are the ones you have to keep and keep happy. Those are the two things I always focus on with anything I'm involved with: What it is trying to do? and who the key people are. Because that is what makes it or breaks it. It is nothing else. A company might be buildings and books and records, but if it doesn't have people every day doing it, it is nothing. That's my advice; focus on those two things; then find your spot there, and treat everybody they way you want to be treated. Then you'll fit in well and do well." (Mr. J. – Utilities)

482.   "I started at the lowest level and I came up through sales and marketing. I got to know every job as I rose through the organization. When I got to a certain point I had to understand other parts of the business such as manufacturing or purchasing. Ultimately, I think you've got to have enough knowledge of the core business so that you understand it well enough that you don't have to fake it. You can't manage what you don't know. Does that make sense? I see a lot of people faking things through life by knowing the buzzwords to say. I can use those buzzwords, but I've always encouraged people to not try to skip levels today to get to the top tomorrow. Serve your time, and do it well in the lower part of the business so you understand it well which will give you the knowledge base you need to have a clear vision and strategy. It will also result in more respect than you'll ever know when you get to the top as CEO. Everybody underneath you will appreciate that you've been there and that you know what they are going through. I think that's crucial." (Mr. E. – Manufacturing)

503.   "My advice is to allow yourself to experience all the different aspects of the business and not get caught up in just what you majored in. Things all kind of blend together in the real world, and even if you're not personally writing up balance sheets, or even if you're not on the floor working on the line, you can bet that at some point in your career – probably more often than you think – you'll need to know what those people are up to, and how their side of the business works. Plus, someday when you're a CEO, you'll need to be able to wear a lot of hats, so you might as well get a head start with that kind of big picture thinking." (Mr. R. – Manufacturing)

510.   "Be able to handle everyday and big picture operations. When I say 'operations' I mean from financial operations, sales operations, general operating strategy, top line, and bottom line functions. It's the essence of being the head of the dog." (Mr. B. – Conglomerate)

525.   "Pay attention to detail, and understand the core elements of your business – every aspect of it." (Mr. W. – Transportation)

529.   "One piece of advice I always tell people is to take a lot of accounting courses. You'll find wherever you are a lot is going to drive around finance and the numbers." (Mr. J. – Utilities)

544.   "No matter what, learn every aspect of the company you work at. Don't just learn about the major you came in with and the job you were hired for. Cross-train a lot and make yourself diverse for the organization. Allow them to see you understanding

what goes on in the company. If you do this, climbing up the ladder will be easier." (Mr. F. – Financial Services)

556. "Whatever businesses you go into, learn the business. Learn what makes it tick. Learn how to operate. Again, you've got to learn the business." (Mr. N. – Energy, Mining & Materials)

567. "You certainly want to gain expertise in an area whether it's finance, marketing, operations, or sales. Whatever it may be, make certain that you have the opportunities – whether on a project basis or otherwise – where you get exposure to other elements of the operation and organization. You don't need to be an expert in every area, but you need to know something about all the different areas. Make certain there are opportunities as you get deep into a discipline that you get the breadth opportunities as well." (Mr. S. – Entertainment & Media)

CAREER DEVELOPMENT

Although no one can justifiably tell you what to do with your life – you must be responsible for your own path, discovering it through your own struggles – yet others certainly can suggest ways to approach that journey. First, find your purpose in life. Second, determine your values and priorities. Then just venture forth, being open to the wonder-filled twists and turns along the way.

25. "MBAs need to work their way up in an organization just like everyone else. I have seen more than a few MBAs believe they are entitled to advancement in a company. However, that is not reality. MBAs first must take what they have learned in their program and apply it to their position within a company, work hard, and results will come with time." (Mr. E. – Manufacturing)

27. "Be very flexible. That's the key to a successful business career. Always be willing to go where the problems are. Most people get married to a location and won't move if asked. If you want to move up in your company just be flexible enough to go anywhere and do anything. When I say do anything, I mean doing things that you think are over your head. You can't be afraid to take on responsibilities that you think you are not ready for." (Mr. M. – Financial Services)

49. "Start your career in a growing industry. There is more chance for success and advancement in a

developing industry rather than one that has been stagnant." (Mr. T. – Information Technology)

52.   "Be yourself as you move up the career ladder because first of all, you cannot be someone else – at least not very well for very long. And, if you will be yourself – with all the character, skills, accomplishments, knowledge, and personality within you – that will get you promoted into areas where people see that you could fit in and perform your best." (Mr. D. – Healthcare)

56.   "Don't be afraid to move around when you're younger. Good experience is transferable among industries and even departments. Good managers show upward mobility, but you have to have your own plan. Always keep it in mind and ask yourself, does the company/position/job/country I am in allow me to fulfill my short-term and long-term objectives? Don't be afraid to leave when it doesn't." (Mr. R. – Manufacturing)

57.   "In order to become a great manager, you must know how to communicate up, down, and across the organization. If you can't gain buy-in and motivate your subordinates, have respect of your peers, and get trust from anyone above you, you can't move into top management spots. So always do unto others as you would have them do unto you. It may seem a little simple, but the Golden Rule can do wonders. Observing this rule can help you earn and keep the respect of employees, customers, and others along your route upward to strategic success." (Mr. D. – Manufacturing)

58.   "When you get a job with a company after you get your degree, you need to get to know the culture of that company and understand what your strengths are and how your strengths can work within that culture to help them succeed and achieve their plan. You should understand that a company would not have hired you if they didn't think you would fit in with the culture, but it is important to understand what the company culture is, so you can contribute to its strategies." (Mr. V. – Business Services)

64.   "Be careful what you ask for because you might get it. Sometimes there may be more to a job than you may see on the front end. So you should do your research and make sure the job you are seeking is what you truly want before you take it." (Mr. T. – Financial Services)

71.   "The hardest part for an individual with an MBA is to calibrate his or her expectations. Over-shooting often times leads to underperforming. In the same way, aiming low can result in missing big. Setting realistic goals and developing a method for accomplishing said goals is a big step in the right direction." (Mr. T. – Hospitality)

73.   "To broaden your development, you need experiences that actively engage your effort and attention for a significant period of time, that push you to think independently and creatively, that ground independent and creative thinking in the classroom training you have already received, and that are challenging enough to make you a little uncomfortable. Focus on developing dedication towards your profession. Focus on studies and learning while at

college. Don't worry about jobs. You will get good jobs if you are dedicated, and earn good grades. At the same time also learn more about present world practices. Don't be too ambitious about your position and pay package in the beginning. Start working and prove your capabilities. Promotion and salary will follow." (Mr. C. – Manufacturing)

79.   "Plan for the future. The only thing that you must understand is that it is imperative to plan your future, whether it be going to school or creating a business plan and implementing it. It is necessary to take time out from everything else to think about where you want to get and how to get there. Do not let the day-to-day activities detract you from what is possibly your most important function – planning for the future." (Dr. T. – Healthcare)

110.   "An MBA is a great door opener, but in the long run no one cares what degree you have. Your work speaks more heavily as you move throughout your career." (Mr. M. – Manufacturing)

115.   "Diversify your employment. In other words, move around to take different jobs when you are starting in the workforce. Part of it is being in the right place at right time, but I do believe you make your own breaks as well though. You must be willing to pay the price; success will not happen overnight." (Mr. W. – Manufacturing)

116.   "I encourage young people in the business world to never feel stuck. Always be looking for a new opportunity that will keep you passionate for your work." (Mr. Z. – Financial Services)

127.   "Being a CEO is not for everybody. Despite the limelight so often portrayed, there is also another side to it, a dark one. Many individuals, and specifically young eager college students, especially those determined to make a difference or climb the corporate ladder, don't distinguish this hidden side of being a CEO." (Mr. C. – Manufacturing)

139.   "None of you will succeed straight out of college barring some massive stroke of luck, simply because you are essentially useless to any corporation. You will be a liability until you prove yourself otherwise, or until the company has invested enough time and money in you to make you useful in whatever way they see fit; and they certainly aren't going to give you top dollar or responsibility of any sort until you have proved to them that you deserve it. A college degree isn't simply going to be enough. You have to do more and work harder than everyone else to prove that you truthfully deserve the right to be in a position. If you don't work hard and have the determination to see your chosen profession to the end, whatever success you achieve will be illusory and may be swept away at any whim of fate." (Mr. C. – Energy, Mining & Materials)

159.   "Be conspicuously inconspicuous. Act like you do not want anyone to know about your great achievements while constantly leaking positive information to key people. This goes a long way in management as well as for personal gain." (Mr. J. – Conglomerate)

162.   "Do not focus on a strict career path. Let the world take you where it may. There are many exciting

possibilities in the career world. Don't be afraid to try them." (Mr. T. – Hospitality)

174. "Hard work really does pay off. But do not focus on what you are going to become. Instead focus on who are you going to work with, because if you choose the wrong people to work with, you career is going to get you into trouble. You should be like a fish in water. It would be a big mistake to start a career which is economically driven." (Mr. S. – Hospitality)

177. "Be energetic and trustworthy, but understand that as you work your way up the organization the best thing that you can do is to make your boss look good." (Mr. C. – Financial Services)

179. "A person may be smart and well educated, and if you put that person in a job he or she would be able to do it. However, if a person really wants to be successful and set themselves apart from others, they need to show that they can provide something special to the organization that it does not already have. They must show that they can bring something to the table that will immediately better the company." (Mr. W. – Entertainment & Media)

193. "Money should not be a priority in choosing a job. Your priority should be placed on the culture of the company and how well you fit into it. You should not go into a job with high expectations because to be successful you need to start at the bottom – to learn about the company – and work your way up." (Mr. H. – Manufacturing)

199.   "Always set goals for yourself and your organization. You should set challenging but realistic goals, have the ability to manage the resources that you have, and realize at what point you may have to change your goals. Most college graduates will not stay at their first job. After your first job, really look and say, 'Is this something that I really want to do?' It is important to know where you want to go in your career, however the goal early on in your career is to find something you're good at and that you enjoy doing." (Mr. C. – Retailing)

200.   "It is important for MBAs coming into a new company to know what the company's overall strategic plan is, and to make sure that they are aligned with it. It's the best career move a person could make – to find projects that fit with the overall strategic plan so that you will have more of an impact and become more noticed." (Mr. V. – Consumer Services)

217.   "Try to work in an area you enjoy. You have to work a long time, so if you're drudging to work in an area you have no interest in, you're unlikely to be good at it. Find that point where your interests match your job. It's okay if you don't know early on, but find where there's a match. Don't be afraid to change what you're doing." (Mr. F. – Construction)

219.   "If you want to advance, do the things other people disregard because they're too difficult or time consuming. Listen. Be persistently patient." (Mr. C. – Business Services)

222.   "The most important piece of advice I can give to a young person is to never be too good for a job. If

a young person wants to be a great leader, they have to be willing to do whatever job is there, even if that job is beneath them. You have to keep in mind that there is never a job that is beneath you. Especially when you're young, you have to get in a job and show that you're willing to do any part of that job." (Mr. M. – Retailing)

226. "You need to find the opinion leaders within the organization. You need to get them on board with what your vision is, and what you want to do. Ultimately, you are the new guy and nobody knows you, but those people have worked there a long time; everyone knows them and listens to them. You have to get those people on board with you because when you start making changes these people will either make it or break it for you. So come in, identify those people, listen to their ideas and tell them your ideas. This will always help new people come in and be accepted." (Mr. S. – Entertainment & Media)

227. "Gain as much experience as you can within different disciplines, different companies, and different industries." (Mr. M. – Hospitality)

229. "Choose your career path carefully. What do you believe you are good at, and what motivates you? What are your interests, and how can those interests, not hobbies, provide you with the means to be successful in life? Next, explore as many options as you can, practically. Be inquisitive; ask a lot of people in a variety of industries about their careers." (Mr. T. – Consumer Products)

230. "What we look for, and people who we pull along, are people who are interested, inquisitive; they're asking questions. They're willing to move along in leadership as they move through the stages of their career. They're willing to tackle tough issues head on. They don't run from a challenge and you'll see that. Some just never quite get there. Especially with the financial condition that we're all in today, it's going to be a real struggle for a lot of us. You know what's kind of the good thing about these times? It's competition. The best people just shine even more in times like these." (Mr. S. – Construction)

236. "In choosing your career path, formulate your own set of goals and aspirations, what you ultimately hope to achieve. In addition to creating a measured guide, it will assist you in identifying the industry or field that motivates you for the sake of the work itself, something to be passionate about apart from money or titles." (Mr. R. – Construction)

238. "Have some personal goals. The last thing you want to do is not know where you want to be five years from now. So many people in life go through without a plan. And that's why I think they blame life on where they are; they don't take the time to sit down and have a personal plan. You have got to do that. Sit down and say, 'Here is where my career is today; here is where I want to be five years from now, and here is what I have to do along the way to get there.' And sometimes putting a five year goal is easy in a sense, because it's five years from now. But you have to back it down to each year. And then you really have to say, 'Okay, today's Friday. My first step is Monday. What am I going to be doing Monday that

starts me down that path?' That's where people stumble. And so you have to have some personal goals. And you have to look for a company that will allow you to be who you are." (Mr. B. – Healthcare)

247. "Go into every interview with full respect for the company and with an excitement for having the ability to work. Show that you have an undying persistence to meet your highest goals, and the company should be quite interested in you." (Mr. W. – Healthcare)

257. "The world is changing so much it makes it hard to figure out your goals and what you want to do. But be particular if you know what you want out of life, if you know what you're good at, or if you know what your dreams are. Chase your dreams; chase your goals. Figure out what you like to do in life. I have a daughter who wanted to be a school teacher; so I told her to teach school for a year and then come back and tell me what she wanted to do. Every summer she came back and said, 'I want to be a school teacher.' Now she's a school teacher. If you know what you really want to do, don't back off; go for it. I wasn't real proud of the school teacher thing; I wanted her to do something else. But she loved her third grade teacher, and she knew exactly what she wanted to do. That's something that's really hard to find. Working hard from the bottom is sometimes what you have to do; taking the right opportunity is what's key. There is so much luck involved. You just have to find something that makes you stand out and go with it. Just chase your dream and do whatever you can to accomplish those dreams. You come out of school you see someone start further up and you have to start at the

bottom; sometimes the person who starts at the top stays there and the person at the bottom works their way up and passes the person who started further up." (Mr. E. – Manufacturing)

260. "Manage your job not your career. As I was rising, I saw people so worried about their careers they forgot about their job. If you manage your current responsibilities well, your career will take care of itself." (Mr. W. – Financial Services)

264. "You need to find your natural inclination. Be honest with yourself and what you feel your strengths are and what you truly want to do. Be honest with yourself – where can I do best? Where will I be the happiest? Where will I be the most comfortable? You must choose something you enjoy and not try to force yourself to be something you are not. It is all about self-honesty. I am not into sales, but I can hire salesmen; I never felt comfortable with sales. It really comes down to being objective about yourself and recognizing what you will be best at." (Mr. W. – Entertainment & Media)

267. "From a personal standpoint I would stay away from large corporations. There is better advancement and personal growth in smaller firms. If I could change anything in my career I would seek out a position in a company owned by an equity group. That can give you a lot of autonomy and personal financial rewards." (Mr. H. – Manufacturing)

269. "I would recommend having some type of career goal planner. I have one to this day and I am 49 years old. It encompasses what am I trying to

accomplish in my marriage, what am I trying to accomplish as a father, what am I trying to accomplish as a business leader, in the community, hobbies, and physical activity goals. I have about three or four things under each one that I track on a quarterly basis to make sure that I am on target with them. I am sure you have probably read this or studied this, but even if you just write it down and never look at again, there is a much higher percent probability that it is going to happen. But if you write it down, whatever it is to you, and then track it on a weekly or monthly basis, the probability that you will succeed in your goals is far greater. But the person that never writes it down and does not really know what is important to him does not really have a path towards success in his career or in his life. It is not necessarily just about his business career. That would be my advice, to have a simple one pager on what is important to you in your life, and what are you going to do to get there. The other point on that is to keep it simple. The simpler you keep a plan, the easier it is to communicate and execute it." (Mr. S. – Manufacturing)

273.   "Well, I think it depends on whether or not you want to start your own business, like I did, or go into corporate America. If you want to succeed in a big company, the best advice I can give would be to become as educated as possible and work your butt off. If you want to be an entrepreneur, I would tell you to start young. The younger you are, the better. When you're young you're willing to put in long hours and aren't worried about anyone but yourself. Actually, I think I'm a cheater entrepreneur. A true entrepreneur is someone who quits a good job while in their forties and chases a wild dream. That's not what I did, I

started young and I think it was a major factor in our success. So depending on what type of career you are looking for, it changes what advice I would give." (Mr. B. – Business Services)

277.   "Remember that you are known by the company you keep, the company you are associated with. You want to be associated with a winner of a company." (Mr. P. – Retailing)

279.   "Look, I have people ask me what it takes to be a CEO, and I tell everybody I really never set out to be a CEO. I always wanted to do the best job that I could at any point in time no matter what I was doing, and I always wanted to do something that I liked and wanted to do. And fortunately things have turned out okay." (Mr. W. – Healthcare)

281.   "I would advise a graduate to look for a career and not a job. In our company, people stay here for a career. We have very low turnover. We take a very long time to decide if we want to hire someone. My advice is to look for a career and not a job. If you are doing that, then you will be happy." (Mr. S. – Consumer Products)

283.   "You're facing a tough job market, number one, but don't get too discouraged about that. I did not appreciate this nearly enough in my career. But as I look back I would say you want to work for organizations that you respect and like, that have expertise and you know you're going to learn from them. And where you can contribute. As you take a position, yes, you want to have the development track. Whether the track is going to be a Chief Financial

Officer, a Chief Marketing Officer, or a Chief Operations Officer, make certain there are opportunities as you get deep into a discipline that you get a breadth opportunities as well." (Mr. S. – Entertainment & Media)

284. "I have people that I work with who know exactly what they want to do. They are not defining jobs, they are defining experiences. Typically they will come to me and say they want to work within this kind of building block managing people. They will say, 'I would like to try working within this other business unit or internationally.' People think about those building blocks. They don't say, 'I want to be a regional manager,' but they clearly begin to think about their career development from an experience standpoint – what they want to have help them develop long term." (Mr. R. – Manufacturing)

290. "To be successful and happy, try to work on something that you believe is important and can make a real and positive difference in the lives of others." (Dr. M. – Healthcare)

291. "We all see the famous quotes, read the books, and watch these specials on the television on how to benchmark yourself and progress in your own career. But the best advice is to write down good advice, bring it to your office, and keep it near you to review frequently." (Mr. B. – Manufacturing)

292. "Jump into the business world and land wherever the wind takes you. During tough economic times everyone should be willing to take any position at any firm because in the end, most likely, you're not

going to finish your career at the same firm that you start at." (Mr. S. – Business Services)

298. "Don't walk out with arrogance. I have an MBA, but don't walk out thinking that you know it all. Back in the 80's, there was a wave of MBAs that came out making a lot of promises, and they screwed up a lot of businesses. They focused on just models, just financials, and didn't focus on creating value. An MBA doesn't make you brilliant; it makes you a fine-tuned, organized thinker and problem-solver. Come out to use those tools to help enhance your organization. You have to use those skills to meet customer needs. Make sure you use those tools that you have gained from the program to enhance yourself. You aren't going to be able to solve all of the problems, but be aware of all of your surroundings. It's a great accomplishment to walk away with an MBA, but you should also come out and say, 'Now, how do I apply this to the betterment of the organization and myself?' Don't sit in your ivory tower with your white shirt, red tie, and blue suit and think you know how to do everything. Take the tools, the talent, and combine it with a focus on your job and the customer. Be patient; it will serve you well. An MBA should make you more flexible if you utilize it well. It will open up doors, but you have to make sure that you don't shut the door behind you. You have to follow through with substance, and then you will go places. Learn the workings of an entire organization, the flexibility of the pathway you want to take, and then take a deep breath. You have the world ahead of you. As you grow in an organization, the higher you get, the more challenging it becomes. You have to be able to deflect the bullets. You will be put into situations where many people want you to

succeed, but a lot of others don't. Make your decisions based on honesty, integrity and professionalism and you will always be on the right path." (Mr. V. – Food & Agriculture)

299.   "Initiative is one of the best traits. If there is a job that you want, act like you already have it." (Mr. D. – Financial Services)

301.   "One other piece of advice I'd give you is this. The word 'entrepreneur' is thrown around a lot, but not everyone is an entrepreneur because not everyone's makeup will allow him or her to be. But if you have that makeup and that burning desire to create something, and you don't mind taking a chance, it can be a very special thing – very rewarding. I once heard a very successful self-made man was asked what it was like to be an entrepreneur. He said that the word that comes to my mind is 'terror.' When I was starting this project – this is not to pat me on the back – I put everything I ever worked for on the line to start this project, all my money and time and effort. I put it on the line. It's not for everybody, but if you have that burning desire, you'll eventually get involved in an opportunity to do something. Obviously if you have that opportunity, you have to have a good work ethic; that goes without saying. All entrepreneurs must have a great work ethic. And it's not for everybody because some people don't want the risk. So often people go into it thinking, 'I'm going to do this and make a lot of money.' But after you actually get into it and you are comfortable where you are, it doesn't become about the money anymore. It becomes that the gratification you feel is more important than money; it's that you care about your people. I know it sounds so cliché but

it's the truth. It's been tried and tested." (Mr. G. – Energy, Mining & Materials)

316.   "Well first of all, have some personal goals. The last thing you want to do is not know where you want to be five years from now. So many people go through life without a plan. And that's why I think they blame where they are on life, but they don't take the time to sit down and have a personal plan. You have got to do that. Sit down and say, 'Here is where my career is today. Here is where I want to be five years from now, and here is what I have to do along the way to get there.' Sometimes setting a five-year goal is easy in a sense because it's five years from now. But you have to back it down to each year. And then you really have to say, 'Okay, today's Friday. My first step is Monday. What am I going to be doing Monday that starts me down that path?' That's where people stumble. And so you have to have some personal goals, and you have to look for a company that will allow you to be who you are." (Mr. B. – Healthcare)

318.   "Know that when you are young and in the early stages of getting out of school and finding that new job, do not become too attached to one company, one organization, or even one career. Pursue new opportunities as they arise, and you will find a career that you want to settle into." (Mr. R. – Energy, Mining & Materials)

324.   "When I went to graduate school at LSU, there was a banker from Southern Mississippi named George, and he had a phrase he used in class: 'When you run an organization there are three things you want to do: feed the horses, shoot the wounded, and keep the herd

together.' That's going to make a successful organization. You figure out who your horses are (the ones that do the heavy lifting and go beyond expectations). You shoot those who are bringing you down and aren't adding value. You keep the organization moving together as a whole and continually shoot for your goals. So, don't ever be the one being shot." (Mr. S. – Financial Services)

327. "Have realistic expectations of what you are capable of doing. Frankly, coming out of school, it almost doesn't matter what school, students believe they are capable of doing a whole lot more than they are. It is simply a function of lacking experience; it doesn't have anything to do with intelligence or hard work." (Mr. H. – Hospitality)

328. "A lot of business is fate and a stroke of luck, especially where you end up. The worst thing you can do is job hop. Do not job hop. Most CEOs and upper managers have been in a company or industry their whole life. You cannot expect to make it to the top right away, or even in five years. You have to be patient and be able to work hard in order to make it to the top." (Mr. B. – Retailing)

329. "Seek more responsibility on your own. Don't wait for it to be given out. Take charge of your career by taking initiative to learn on your own. Be open-minded and constantly seek out constructive criticism. Be persistent, and focus on doing your best even in a difficult environment. You will have disappointments and unjust situations occur along the way. But do not lose your patience, confidence and integrity. Stay the course, and eventually the cream will rise to the top.

Do not stay and quit in your heart. If you are that frustrated, leave and do something that is a better fit." (Mr. B. – Retailing)

330. "There is no perfect company or perfect job. Your job or career is what you make of it. So, that means that you cannot stop learning. Keep reading, learning about the industry, looking for ways to grow personally." (Mr. S. – Healthcare)

332. "One does not start as a CEO – unless your family gives it to you – so work in different departments to horizontally grow. Most CEOs are selected because of their background in many different areas of business: finance, sales, customer service, etc." (Ms. R. – Information Technology)

341. "If you come to the conclusion that you are happy with your life: 'I like my life; I like this money, and I like this job,' that's fine too. There is nothing wrong with that. Not everybody is going to be President; they are just not. But if you want to, don't set your sights too low. And if you feel comfortable, or you get to the point where you feel comfortable right here – 'Life is great; I don't want that up there,' that is fine too. That's like saying every kid has to go to college. I wish every kid could go to college, but they don't have to." (Mr. D. – Retailing)

342. "When you are looking around at what you want to do and where you want to find employment, focus on the culture of the company; it will tell you everything. You must know what you are in it for. If it is only for the money, then it is probably a bad idea. You must be involved in something that you get a

reward out of, that you enjoy." (Mr. H. – Consumer Products)

345. "My advice would be to find something that you are good at and that you enjoy, and then find a way to incorporate those into your work. My degree was in Finance and Accounting. That doesn't mean that I enjoy doing all the financials. Actually I hate it. I wouldn't have made a good CPA because that's not really what I enjoy. I love the personal aspect of my job, working with people. So you have to know what it is you like to do and what you're good at. I also think it's important that you go back to school if you can. Even if you have to borrow the money or go to school at night it would be worth it to your career. Having an MBA would really help set you apart from the other guys, especially for kids your age. Everybody has a four-year degree. Graduate programs are really beneficial, more so than four-year programs. They really teach you a lot more about being successful in business. I really enjoyed the MBA program when I was in it." (Mr. B. – Financial Services)

352. "Don't worry much about title or salary when starting out a career. Look for a stable, growing company and a leader that will give you the opportunity to grow and develop. You may have heard the expression that 'People don't leave companies; they leave leaders.' I've found that to be very true. Evaluate your potential leader, and as many others at your prospective employer as possible, because you will likely change supervisors multiple times. I also believe that working for an employer with a strong brand early in your career will benefit you much more in the future than the fact that you made

an extra $2 per hour or had a fancy title. For example, 20 years down the road, hiring managers won't care that you started at an entry level. They will see the name of the firm and want to know about the culture and the customer service. Or you might take a job out of college as a District Manager for NoName Company to make a little more money, but in the long run you may not have the same opportunities." (Mr. K. – Transportation)

355. "Understand your strengths and you weaknesses. A person who is just starting into their career needs to lean toward their strengths, but always strengthen his or her weaknesses. You can always impress an interviewer by knowing yourself and by showing a willingness to learn. Once you do reach a management position, you need to remember to hire with the intention of counteracting your own weaknesses." (Mr. K. – Energy, Mining & Materials)

355. "Someone always needs to establish themselves before entering into their parent's business because that is the only way to gain respect upon entry into the business. I am making my children work somewhere else first before they come work for me." (Mr. K. – Energy, Mining & Materials)

359. "Don't be discouraged by 'redundant work' and long hours. Those are jobs that need to get done by someone. If you're not going to do it, someone else will. People who take on assignments no matter how tedious will eventually be trusted with greater responsibility." (Mr. J. – Healthcare)

386. "Be willing to relocate, embrace your company, participate in community activities, be gutsy – like requesting time with the current CEO – pursue higher learning and education, demonstrate enthusiasm and passion, and don't forget to balance work and life." (Mr. S. – Utilities)

393. "Don't be concerned that your first job might not be the job you wanted five years ago. Remember you have to learn the job bottom up. Most people have multiple jobs through their lifetimes. Don't be afraid to use your entrepreneurial skills either. Start a side business while you are working your job. Great companies start off as small companies. Do not plan to start at the top." (Mr. L. – Consumer Products)

399. "Another thing I would try to do in your position is simply visit lots of companies. Look for a way to go in and walk around to see what people do. If you haven't been through our factory, you should because it is one of the most interesting in the world. Customers come in here and they are blown away. I would look for the opportunity just to pick out five people you know and ask to take a tour of their company and get a feel for how things work. I never did that. I came here straight out of college and have been here ever since. It was a really poor decision I made. I didn't bring anything to the table when I started but a strong work ethic. I didn't really know anything and had no experience related to the job I came into. It would be much more interesting to get different types of experience and see many different things as a college graduate to get a feel for how business works. This doesn't mean work 100 places,

but try to at least see 100 places." (Mr. F. – Manufacturing)

401. "I feel so sorry for the people who get up in the morning, and they dread going to work. It is so sad, and an issue a strategic manager cannot solve. So you really need to find something that you feel good about. Maybe you're aligned with a company philosophically, in terms of with what they are trying to achieve, or even what you want to do with your life. I've been very fortunate to work with a lot of people I've respected, and you spend a lot of time with the people you work with. You probably spend more waking hours with them than with your own family. It needs to be someplace where you are comfortable and it is the right fit. And if it is not the right fit, you will know either that the type of business is not right for you, or that particular place is not right for you. You will be able to feel it. An organization that is not right for the employee or the employer is miserable." (Mr. M. – Energy, Mining & Materials)

401. "Employers like to hear about people who have ambition, and are interested in trying something different, something new to raise the bar. So if you work hard, constantly seek challenges, and then a certain amount of luck is involved – being in the right place, at the right time, in the right situation – you will have success." (Mr. M. – Energy, Mining & Materials)

407. "Don't be in a hurry to make money or climb the corporate ladder. Live your life and do the things you always dreamed of doing since you were a little kid, and all the rest will take care of themselves as long as you work hard." (Mr. U. – Entertainment & Media)

414.   "I tell my kids all the time that they will have five or six jobs throughout their lifetimes, so never stop learning because you don't know what you'll be doing next. And don't burn any bridges because that could be the next job you want, or the next client that you have. And learn Spanish or Chinese." (Mr. M. – Healthcare)

421.   "You need to be patient. The employee who is well educated and performs well, works hard, puts in the extra hours, and communicates clearly will go a long way in any company. You must contribute to the company in any way possible. Offer well thought out suggestions, and be honest. Present yourself as a package deal with some edginess and you will not go unnoticed. Try to be yourself, and always show respect." (Mr. R. – Financial Services)

429.   "Clearly, the first job you have is likely to not be the last job you will have. I see resumes from people who have eight, ten, or twelve previous employers. That is very different from two or three decades ago. The reason for this change is that we are a much more mobile society, and information is more accessible and flows more freely which is a good thing. You should find something that you love to do with a company that reflects the values that you have. Work hard and then be patient about getting a promotion. You should look for your opportunity to advance and be ready to take that opportunity when it arises. On the flip side, I've had people tell me that they are ready to advance when they are not because they are impatient. But more times than not, we meet with someone to give them a promotion or raise that they weren't expecting,

and those are some of my favorite days." (Mr. R. – Construction)

430.   "Become a master at what you do. Do it to the best of your abilities. Seek to broaden your skill set. I think back to when I started, I was always trying to get involved in a new project, to cut my teeth on something new. I've seen people who just stay stuck. Those people who advance tend not to be satisfied in the day-to-day. You have to look beyond the dashboard of what you're doing." (Mr. R. – Consumer Products)

433.   "Do not ever be ashamed of what you do not know; stay curious; find your passion, and ask for feedback. There is nothing wrong with asking for a review three months after you have started a position, asking if there is anything you can be doing better, anything you need to stop doing." (Ms. T. – Consumer Products)

434.   "I believe very strongly, that you should take a job almost anywhere that you can get with a large, well managed company. It will better position you for long term career success." (Mr. H. – Hospitality)

440.   "I challenge you do to new and exciting stuff. Do things you actually like, not what will pay the most income. Look around and take opportunities. If you get a chance to work or study in other states or overseas, do it! Just remember that you're going to start out low on the totem pole in your career. My first job was in sales, much different from what I do now. You'll learn though that all kinds of experience is what

will make you a great leader." (Mr. S. – Consumer Products)

442. "I don't care if you get a job in the mail room, call center, or on the front lines selling product or services. A lot of people get out of school and spend the first three to five years at what they think are dead end jobs because they never broadened themselves to think through any further than where they were." (Mr. C. – Entertainment & Media)

442. "An important question is, 'How do you transition from all that studying into the workplace?' Find a job not a career. You can work on your career while you're in a job. By that I mean focus on furthering yourself in the company that you're in. Then you can jump off or start your own company." (Mr. C. – Entertainment & Media)

444. "Who you're with is more important than what you do. Don't get out of college and tell someone that you want to work for one hundred grand a year. It's nice to get that, but only if it's around people that you really like, that you respect, that you want to be like. I would rather have a ten thousand dollar job around someone that I liked and respected than a hundred thousand dollar job around someone that I didn't. I think that that is so important." (Mr. C. – Financial Services)

446. "Patience is the key when beginning your career. So often young people think that once they get into a job things will progress at a very rapid pace. For many it doesn't move that fast at all. You must pick a good business or industry. You can enter a bad business and

no matter how talented or good you are, you may never move up the ladder limiting your options. So find an employer with good training programs, such as Procter & Gamble or Johnson & Johnson. These programs are very beneficial to those young in their careers. Financial services firms have very formal training programs. A lot of people have gone through those, and in two or three years they are working elsewhere but take that skill set with them for other opportunities." (Mr. B. – Manufacturing)

449.   "Don't let anyone tell you what you should do, and don't pick a career because someone else that you respect and love did the same thing! Pick a career that you enjoy. Trust me, it will make all of the difference in the world." (Mr. M. – Consumer Services)

450.   "Early in your career try to experience as many different facets of your business as you can. Experience working in a variety of venues. Doing so will make you very well-rounded, and it will keep you very marketable – very valuable." (Ms. B. – Food & Agriculture)

451.   "It took me 35 years to get where I am today, so you must be patient, try a lot of different things, and not get pigeon holed in one specific area. Create broad-based experiences across all disciplines of your industry. Get a feel for the day-to-day running of operations, sales, finance and marketing." (Mr. R. – Financial Services)

454.   "The most important thing to remember in starting a career is to make sure that your job is something you look forward to each morning when

you get out of bed. The career path you choose needs to be interesting and challenging so that you can grow and become a better person." (Mr. W. – Financial Services)

464. "Don't expect to find something great overnight. Be flexible in where you work and what you want to make. Know what direction you want to head. Do whatever you would enjoy the most. Focus on what you want to do, and go that direction. It will be a very steep hill for a while, but be patient. It's a grind right now. When the tide's out, the tide's out. Nothing can make it come in. Recognize where you are. Do your best and be realistic. And network as best you can; it all comes down to people." (Mr. H. – Construction)

471. "Work for good organizations, those that treat their people well, their vendors well, that treat all their constituents, all their stakeholders, really well. You have to go to a place that has a great reputation. If you want to go into marketing, clearly Procter & Gamble would have to be one of the companies that you want to have on your list. If you want to go into the airline business, Southwest Airlines would be one that you want on your list. Large industrial companies, something like General Electric. Computer companies, something like Apple or IBM. These are people that have been around a long time and have demonstrated good success over time. Coca-Cola is another great company. PepsiCo, another great company. You know they're going to take the best and the brightest, and they're going to be thinking about their objectives, and they want to measure their success with a longer term view. You really do need to attach yourself with the

best organization you can find, one that demonstrates the kind of success you want to have. And make sure you work for companies where you know you will continue your learning, and that will also give you the chance to take on more responsibility over time which will put you in a position to have an impact on strategic thinking." (Mr. O. – Hospitality)

483.   "Be passionate about what you are doing, or don't move forward. Be innovative, creative, and don't be afraid to take risks. Bring something unique to your industry, something that will set you apart from others. Seek mentors; never stop learning; don't overextend your resources, and most of all, have fun!" (Ms. F. – Manufacturing)

490.   "When you get out of school, don't worry about getting the best job in the world. Worry about getting a job where you can learn and realize that you are going to need to make some changes and sacrifices. I would always do more than expected; under-promise and over-deliver. Always keep your word, and be very loyal to your boss. I would never criticize my boss to anyone else. If you want to talk bad about your boss, only do it to your dog because it will get back to them. Always be polite; always treat people right; do what you say you'll do, and what you'll find is people will take care of you. They don't want to see you get hurt. But if you act like you know everything and you're sharp with people, they will want to cut your legs off. I would say always keep a good attitude. Leave your baggage at home when you walk in the door. If you want to bitch about something, be careful who you bitch to. Don't be afraid to say, 'I don't know, but I'll find out.' I would be amazed if you knew exactly what

you want to do. Don't be ashamed about that. If you want something, you're going to have to pay the price." (Mr. R. – Healthcare)

492. "Do what you enjoy doing, let interests pull you the direction they pull. Don't be too analytical; don't calculate the financial rewards. Enjoy the career path you are on. Life is too short." (Mr. L. – Transportation)

495. "Probably the most important aspect is that the culture of the firm should align with your core values as best as possible. It will never perfectly match up, but you want to make sure there is a close enough fit so you can feel comfortable in that environment and perform to the best of you ability." (Mr. S. – Information Technology)

496. "Don't be in a hurry when you get in your career; we live a long time. We are living longer than ever now and you will be around awhile. Life happens, so take it slow." (Mr. B. – Healthcare)

498. "I would say put together a personal development program. Work with your supervisor on how you can continue to grow. Start to set or redefine your objectives for yourself. Learn all you can and just continue to move forward and support your company; good things will happen. I am very focused throughout the company with personal development plans; that is so critical. Try to take different jobs in the company so you broaden your skill set. I just had someone move from merchandising to distribution, as an example. And I moved someone from sourcing to merchandising because I want to broaden their capabilities so they can

be stronger and can actually do an even better a job for the company over time." (Mr. M. – Manufacturing)

501.   "When you start your career, find the company with the absolute best system for developing its people. It does not matter what job you take; I'd mop floors if it were necessary. You are better off starting lower and working your way up than taking a higher position where you may not grow as much in the long term." (Mr. H. – Manufacturing)

504.   "I would try to find a top-notch company that has a really good development program for their people and work for them even if you have to start by scrubbing their floors if that's how you have to get in. Find a company that is good at that, and work your way from the ground up." (Mr. Z. – Manufacturing)

505.   "You must have some type of competitive advantage; you must have special talents or attributes that you can offer to the company. You must stand out in a way that is different from other prospects." (Ms. L. – Consumer Products)

506.   "Be willing to accept whatever work is offered. Get your foot in the door, and then show them what you are made of." (Mr. H. – Financial Services)

510.   "If I were you, I would move. I decided to leave my hometown for 3 or 4 years before I went back and made it my home for good. Understand how the rest of the world works, and what it means to become an international thinker. Do it while you are still young." (Mr. B. – Conglomerate)

516.   "My father used to tell me a story about a gentleman from Tennessee in the scrap business. He was good at it and he could make a lot of money in it, but it didn't have much respect in the community. So he would venture out and try this and that, but it just never worked out. And he would end up coming right back to the scrap business. Finally he said, 'I've learned my lesson and I am staying right here.' He had a passion for the business. Had he not been so concerned with how people saw him, he could have made the scrap business a much better trade. Now that was early recycling and we need people like him to perfect these industries. Does it matter that they are not glamorous? Not one bit." (Mr. H. – Retailing)

520.   "There are so many avenues to be successful; you can choose anything. I never expected to be in this business; I originally knew nothing about it. It just shows that you never have to be stuck into one industry or job. Just find yourself."   (Mr. B. – Manufacturing)

527.   "It is always greener somewhere else, meaning there is always somebody that is going to be doing better than you are doing. And you can look at them and say, 'Gosh, I have to switch jobs because I want to be like Joe Blow.' But really you don't know if Joe is happy or not. He could be the meanest, most unhappy person underneath. Every job has its ups and downs. And by the end of the month or end of the year you have to be able to look back and say, 'I thrive.' We all can't be CEOs of companies, but we can still be successful with an organization and be satisfied and provide a good living for ourselves and our family.

Hopefully you will have a real open mind to what you want to do." (Mr. J. – Manufacturing)

539. "Experiment in order to get a wide range of experiences as soon as possible. Don't get too set in your ways in having to find a 25-year place of employment right off the bat. You have to spread your wings and get into unique and different opportunities so that you can see different perspectives, different ways of doing things, and different ways of accomplishing things." (Mr. M. – Hospitality)

542. "No job is menial. Be the best janitor, mail carrier, or project manager you can be, and take pride in your work. People will always notice." (Mr. D. – Construction)

546. "A CEO's job is full-time; it's something you think about all day every day. You go on vacation and you still think about it. You think about it when you go to bed at night. There's very little break from it; it's not just 40 hours a week. Even when you're not at work it is always on your mind." (Mr. R. – Consumer Products)

547. "Your first job most likely will not be your dream job. Be willing to take on jobs that don't seem exciting to you. The opportunity to learn from that first 'boring' job is crucial to your career, whatever it may be. Also, if you want to get ahead and distinguish yourself from the pack, you must come in early and stay late. Everyone will take notice – in a good way!" (Mr. L. – Energy, Mining & Materials)

549. "Stay focused on doing the best job you can in your current job. Also, always be someone that can be counted on to do what they committed to do when they committed to it. Bring a positive attitude to work every day. Strive to do a good job, and always look to learn and improve. Take pride in your work and company. Be a team player, and always try to follow good ethics; those are important. (Mr. F. – Manufacturing)

553. "Know that you might have to start lower than you want to get into the industry you want. Do your best with whatever job you get, and if you really do the best you can, people will notice. They will see what you are doing and know there is something different about you. Be patient and work as hard as you can." (Mr. H. – Financial Services)

556. "If you are working for somebody, you are there for one reason – to make them money." (Mr. N. – Energy, Mining & Materials)

560. "Whenever you interview for a position with a company, ask them questions; interview them back because you want to make sure they have the culture you want to work in. You should want to know if they respect their people and if you feel comfortable in that environment. Ask a lot of questions and get to know what they're all about so there won't be any surprises." (Mr. C. – Entertainment & Media)

566. "The question always has to be – if you want to be successful in any endeavor – the question has to be, 'What can you do for the company, not what the

company can do for you?' to paraphrase a great President." (Dr. S. – Manufacturing)

CHANGE AND FLEXIBILITY

Some of us say, "I don't like change. I'm not good with change." Change is indeed costly, risky, threatening – and it is vital. Life itself depends on change. But the assurance is that we do not have to compromise what matters most – our purpose, our dreams, our values, our priorities. But we certainly will not survive long or thrive unless we do adapt our ways of approaching those things that matter most. And in that we find life.

53.   "One can never get too comfortable with a 'just keep doing what worked before' type of attitude. I want you to know that just because something worked at first does not mean it will always work. Strategic management is not an exact science; you have to react to the ever-changing conditions that are brought to you. Planning is great, but in the end it's just a plan." (Mr. C. – Retailing)

104.   "Management continually evolves. It is dynamic and changes all the time. Most of these changes are caused by external forces that you cannot control. Sometimes things that did work before will not in the future, so one has to be able to adjust in order to be useful and add value in your current circumstances." (Mr. V. – Business Services)

106.   "Strategic management is so big that it is never done; it is a never-ending story. Whatever you write down one day, it will be different the next. It is not a

finished product; it is constantly being molded." (Mr. S. – Manufacturing)

111. "Be consistent. Managers can get themselves into sticky situations when they are not consistent. You should be consistent with your employees, your customers, your colleagues, and all other entities with which you deal regularly." (Mr. B. – Real Estate)

116. "Always be ready and eager to change direction. I must emphasize the importance of maintaining a high level of focus after a change of direction as well. Many young managers are flexible, but not many can balance flexibility and focus. This is something I look for in young talent." (Mr. Z. – Financial Services)

140. "Never lose sight of your objectives, but do change the way of getting there." (Mr W. – Real Estate)

146. "In my years of experience, another possible trap I have noticed MBAs fall into is the trap of a rigid strategic plan. When many MBAs first get the opportunity to create a strategic plan they make one that is extremely rigid and in the process fall in love with it. What they need to know is that it is okay to map out a strategy and plan, but you have to reevaluate it and be willing to make changes if necessary. In fact, I recommend only planning ahead about one year, and then reevaluating all plans, maybe even sooner if possible." (Mr. G. – Food & Agriculture)

169. "The environment in which an organization operates is not static. Because of this, you must keep your headlights on high beam so that your organization is positioned to be responsive, not

reactive. In other words, strategically understand the potential for change in your environment." (Mr. T. – Healthcare)

186. "Enjoy uncertainty. An inability to accept uncertainty as a reality in business may equate to an inability to sleep at night. Those who are truly successful in leadership tend to effectively differentiate between uncertainty versus a lack of understanding. Obtaining knowledge can give us understanding, but we can only cope with the presence of uncertainty." (Mr. Y. – Consumer Services)

190. "Great strategic plans do not equal success. Success will come with adaptation and work. It is important for a company to have a process and strategic direction, but one should not focus exclusively on this. Strategy isn't everything. Flexibility is." (Mr. D. – Biotechnology)

197. "Strategic management is unique to each industry and can be different for each company within a particular industry. It is a process, not an end result. Strategic management is dynamic and changes constantly. Because of the changing nature of business and strategic management, it needs to be addressed by senior management on an ongoing basis. What worked last year or even six months ago may not be what works six months from now or next year." (Mr. D. – Manufacturing)

203. "Understand that strategic management is a very thoughtful, information gathering, consensus building, clearly defined process. Once a plan has been developed, you need to always recognize that it has to

be flexible enough, as there are often times external forces that are not in your control that might force changes. You must be able to enhance and modify and manage through those changes to have a direction that will succeed." (Ms. H. – Financial Services)

213.   "Firms can never let their guard down. If a firm is to survive in the long-term and maintain its profitability, they have to be in touch with their environment at all times. Managers should have antennae for changes in competition, customer trends and also regulations."   (Mr. B.   –   Information Technology)

219.   "Business plans are dynamic and can be and are often revised during the execution phase of the plan. So review the plan often; do not be too rigid to change the plan. And if the plan is failing, first discover the reasons for the failed plan and then adjust as necessary." (Mr. C. – Advertising)

229.   "Be flexible and adaptable. The world's always changing; you have to be able to foresee and to change with the times."   (Mr. T. – Consumer Products)

232.   "Be flexible. I read somewhere recently where today's graduates are going to go through several different occupational changes during their career span. So, be willing to move around between industries as the opportunity arises and take those things that you learned from past experiences, and apply those that will help you and learn new ones as you go along." (Mr. S. – Healthcare)

237.   "Set a direction and adjust it as you go. I think the best analogy is, if you're a sailor on the sea, you set your course where you want to go, but it depends on how the wind blows. You can't set your sails exactly how you want. You set them as near to what you want as you can, and then you correct them as you go. There is no way to sit in your port and work out the exact route you're going to take; it doesn't work like that." (Mr. S. – Consumer Products)

261.   "Change is painful and not easy, but generally necessary for success and happiness in a long-term sense. Accept that you will not always be in control and cannot predict everything." (Mr. F. – Financial Services)

262.   "Plan. But always have a constant update of the plan. Be able to see your markers of success. Plan from point A to point B, but do not be discouraged by ambiguity." (Mr. C. – Healthcare)

286.   "Knowledge is power. But, add to your knowledge a readiness to adapt to situations quickly. To be able to do this, build strong networks with people early on. Most of all, open your heart and mind to welcome change." (Mr. V. – Information Technology)

337.   "Once you put together the greatest strategy in the world, it will change tomorrow. The real successful managers and companies are the ones that know how to react to the strategy when things change around them." (Mr. T. – Information Technology)

341.   "Plans need to be living, breathing documents, not carved in stone. They need to be reviewed on a continuous basis, re-forecasted, re-analyzed, and refined based on the information that keeps coming back to you. I think a lot of times people think this is the way you plan: once you plan it, this is the way you do it. But be willing to change that plan, even a strategic plan, but not at every whim, not the main part, not even the end result, but possibly the details within the plan. You created some strategies to get to this result, and you realize that some of them aren't quite right so you need to tweak this one or that one." (Mr. D. – Retailing)

390.   "There are certain elements of strategic management that are universal, but when you get on the job, flexibility becomes very important – being able to be flexible to the point of reacting to your environment, reacting to the marketplace, reacting to the economy. That changes your strategic intent a lot of times. So you'd have to be dedicated to the fundamentals because the fundamentals will be constants, but realize that the implementation has to be flexible. A lot of times you have to scratch your whole approach and start over again because it doesn't always work out as you plan." (Mr. B. – Consumer Products)

393.   "No matter what you do, some things will be outside of your control. All you can do is your best, plan the best as you can, and be ready to react." (Mr. L. – Consumer Products)

403.   "Every business needs a plan; the discipline of planning is worthwhile. But while some direction is

needed, we do not worship the plans. They need to be changed very often." (Mr. G. – Energy, Mining & Materials)

419. "No matter what industry or company you work for there is going to be a constant learning curve. This goes hand-in-hand with constant change. I like that our company is 101 years old; there is a lot of history to it, but there is a lot of change. We're going through a lot of change right now which is great." (Ms. B. – Consumer Services)

452. "Change is the only thing we know is going to happen. So one always needs to be looking forward and planning ahead. The really successful organizations are the ones who have mastered this." (Ms. A. – Biotechnology)

459. "Strategic management is an evolving process. You have to be open-minded and willing to change." (Mr. B. – Financial Services)

462. "Once you've determined your destination and you know where you are today, then the question becomes 'How can I get from A to B?' The important thing is that on any journey you're likely to take a detour. But that detour is not in the least bit worrisome if you know where you're trying to get back to and where that destination is." (Mr. B. – Consumer Products)

475. "Without strategic management in today's highly competitive marketplace, it would be hard to survive. Knowing what your strengths, weaknesses, opportunities and threats are, and knowing how to use,

overcome or take advantage of them is essential. Strategic planning not only sets a direction for your business, but it also gives guidance on how to get there. However, today's leaders must realize that strategic plans do not last as long as in the past. With sudden changes in the economy, new products, new delivery channels and the rapid changes in technology, strategic plans must be reviewed on a regular basis so that management will stay on top of its game and not be left behind." (Mr. W. – Financial Services)

550. "Adaptability is a very important quality in management, especially when a crisis occurs. You must continually find different methods of solving problems or resolving situations. Never forget that every assignment is a chance to learn and adapt or update your skill set as well. Take advantage of every opportunity to take on new challenges and experiences; you will appreciate the knowledge you gain from those experiences later." (Mr. T. – Consumer Services)

663. "The only thing constant in the real world of management is change, and that change occurs in real-time. Many times changes occur without the benefit of a notice or warning." (Mr. D. – Energy, Mining & Materials)

COMMUNICATION AND LISTENING

Of course we all know by now that for more than a generation the skill that employers say they want most in those they hire is "communication skills." Do you take that to mean giving speeches? Listen...

11.   "What helps people to become excellent, but not perfect, is to always be open-minded and closed-mouthed. Listen more than you speak; be polite, respectful and professional." (Mr. M. – Retailing)

18.   "Stay humble and listen to others. Listening skills are just as important, if not more, than speaking skills." (Mr. A. – Financial Services)

29.   "You need to understand and have a good grasp of the human side of business to be able to get your ideas across. I believe that in order to be successful you have to be a good salesman to others of your ideas in order for others to buy into them. There are a lot of great thinkers who cannot communicate their ideas." (Mr. D. – Energy, Mining & Materials)

50.   "It's all about people and communicating with them regularly, completely, thoroughly. You need to listen to what they have to say and respect their thoughts, opinions, ideas, etc." (Dr. C. – Healthcare)

51.   "Effective communication is all about building trust. That is the key thing." (Dr. M. – Healthcare)

56.   "Management is all about communication. You have to communicate, communicate and communicate. But everybody knows that, right? The secret is how to communicate and with whom. You've got to act like you are really listening and understanding, because you should. But, almost as important, you have to show it! People need to see and feel it in you. They will instantly connect to you if you do this. They will seek you out, recommend you, and talk about you to their peers and superiors. You have to be a very approachable person, one that is very easy to talk to. You've got to talk to everybody. Everybody deserves your time and respect. Even the cleaning lady is your good friend." (Mr. R. – Manufacturing)

66.   "You must be an excellent communicator. But most of all, become a good listener. Develop your question and answer skills; ask questions until you're satisfied. Don't do something you think you know how to do just because you're afraid to ask questions." (Mr. F. – Financial Services)

77.   "Communication and writing skills are what got me to this position." (Mr. R. – Financial Services)

101.   "Learn to listen. When you graduate and get your diploma, it gives you the privilege of listening and asking questions. While your education does not endow you with a tremendous amount of knowledge, it should give you a better sense of what questions to ask and the right people to ask." (Mr. B. – Entertainment & Media)

111.   "Learn how to communicate effectively. This goes hand in hand with building relationships. A

manager must be able to communicate effectively in order to be a success. This includes such things as knowing when to praise work, knowing when to take blame for a mistake, knowing how to effectively communicate how a job should be done, and knowing the best time and method for critiquing someone's work. I feel that one of the reasons that I have been successful is that I have always tried to be an effective communicator." (Mr. B. – Real Estate)

115.   "Communication, communication. Don't ever let your ego talk for you." (Mr. W. – Manufacturing)

118.   "Good communication is key to a successful business; it helps keep everyone informed, and it allows us to make changes as soon as they are needed." (Mr. M. – Hospitality)

157.   "Communicate effectively. Someone out there has the answer you're looking for; you just need to find a way to get it out of them." (Mr. A. – Utilities)

160.   "One mandatory skill that I believe all people must develop is communication skills, particularly in written communication. I find even in my own organization that there are few people who are good writers. Terribly unorganized, rambling emails are a major problem. I require emails sent to me to contain full sentences, not just a flood of disconnected words. I believe that the elements required to be a good writer center primarily on critical thinking and organization. You must go through a particular process when writing. First, communicate the facts and issues. Then discuss the mission and objectives. Finally, communicate how to go about executing those plans. If someone is a very

effective communicator, they can move up in the organization." (Mr. M. – Entertainment & Media)

172.   "Be a story teller! After 25 years of experience, telling stories about business and projects that have occurred in the office or in the field has made a huge difference in my career. Stories sell! The stories do not need to be success stories; in fact, they can be of failures or of just about anything. In the end it makes employees, and especially customers, feel more like they are part of the history and culture of the company." (Mr. Z. – Energy, Mining & Materials)

173.   "Learn to listen. Too many MBAs think they know everything and don't think they still need to learn. Education is not everything. By listening to executives in your organization you will learn the other part to being a valuable employee or manager. This will enable you to be able to see clearly, think broadly, and act strategically." (Mr. M. – Information Technology)

202.   "Listening. This is something that can be applied far beyond the work environment. I am a huge advocate of listening to the people you interact with, from your employees to your family, your spouse and friends. In addition to the need to listen is the need to ask the right questions to get the information you want or need. Remember important listening thoughts like, 'What are the people I am talking to saying? What are they really saying?' It is this type of thing that allows two things to happen. One, people will begin telling you more because you listen; and two, you will begin getting the information you really need." (Mr. N. – Entertainment & Media)

270.   "Listen. I see this all the time: a kid will come in with a job in sales and all he wants to do is vomit out the brochure he's been trained to know. That's not being you. Listening helps you understand the wants and needs of the person that you're talking to and helps build integrity, which in the end, that's all that people want. Early on in your career it is so hard to listen because you're so excited, but you must remember to be yourself and to listen and actually hear what someone has to say. You can learn more from a customer, an account, or any other person from listening rather than speaking." (Mr. Z. – Healthcare)

287.   "Also important is a focus on communication skills. Those are the skills that I think are most important for anyone that is trying to move into a senior executive position. I think that means being able to write well and write concisely in order to articulate points effectively using the fewest amounts of words with the greatest amount of clarity." (Mr. G. – Manufacturing)

311.   "The only advice I have always given staff is to understand the client, the person at the other side of the table. Be it a customer, or a peer, or a subordinate, try to figure out their side of the conversation. Understand what they are thinking; understand what they are trying to do, what they are trying to achieve in the situation. It usually gives you a much better position. If you understand what your client, competitor and staff are doing, it gives you a better way of positioning your opinion or your goal." (Mr. G. – Business Services)

322.   "The first thing out of the gate that will be the most beneficial to you is communication skills. I have seen people with brilliant ideas, but they just cannot get them communicated, and that really hurts in the long run. Of course it depends on the kind of position you are in, but my experience is that we are always selling. You are always selling your ideas and selling your concepts. So if you are going to make an impact, you have to continue selling. Some people will tell you they are in R&D or Accounting, so 'I don't have to sell.' Baloney! You have to sell to people who are making all kinds of decisions. You may not know you are selling, but you always are. So I think that going in having good communication skills is a huge benefit. I know everybody today likes to get on email or use text messages, but it's not any less important to be able to communicate. The younger generation is taking that for granted. It is becoming more and more rare to find people capable of and willing to engage face-to-face, verbally, thinking on your feet, having quick responses to challenges and issues. Those skills are hugely important for developing your personal competitive advantages early in a career, and even where I am today. I have been in management for thirty-one years, and I still have to do it. I think a generation is losing that skill. I have on several occasions had employees sitting next to each other who will send an email or text rather than engage with each other. I am not really sure why they just don't talk, but I think this is an illustration of the direction this diminishing skill is headed." (Mr. C. – Food & Agriculture)

365.   "One of things I always emphasize is the importance of knowing how to communicate. One of the most important ways you have to communicate is

by listening. We don't listen enough. I always try to make it a point to listen. Before you communicate you need to listen to what your customers are saying, and what your employees are saying. If you are just communicating and not speaking to the issues because you did not listen, then you are not accomplishing anything. So listen." (Mr. M. – Utilities)

398. "Most successful CEOs are good listeners. Listening skills are extremely important to someone who has just come into an organization and is a student." (Mr. R. – Consumer Products)

401. "You cannot communicate enough, but it needs to be meaningful. It can't be hollow or phony. There is a reason everyone gathers around the water cooler, or goes to the coffee bar and chats stuff up. It is because they want information. People want to know more. What you really need to do is communicate as many facts as you can, so everyone understands what is going on and what is expected." (Mr. M. – Energy, Mining & Materials)

482. "I always believe that I learn more when I'm in difficult times. When I'm in good times I want to talk more than I want to listen. I think that is another key thing people need, to be a wonderful listener. You learn a lot more by listening." (Mr. E. – Manufacturing)

656. "Listening to others will broaden your own views." (Mr. E. – Utilities)

668. "The secret to success in business is being short and to the point. It is important to boil things down and not waste others' time." (Mr. T. – Retailing)

CREATIVITY AND INNOVATION

Some say that creativity cannot be taught. Some say that they were not "born" creative. Whether or not those are true, the world is indeed calling for new and different approaches. If you want to be outstanding, you must stand out. If you want to make a difference, you must be different. Try moving your focus away from what you are or are not. That's not the point of life or of business. The key is to move our focus toward what others need and want. Play!

60.   "One of the things that makes us successful is our refusal to follow the crowd. We are almost completely contrarian. I urge the same type of attitude in aspiring executives. I blame a herd mentality for many of the bad decisions that are made in the business world. After all, if you fail when all others are failing, there is a built-in excuse, so there are strong disincentives for creating original, unique opportunities. As a result, business leaders move en masse from one extreme to the next." (Mr. C. – Financial Services)

163.   "It is important that you stand out from among the group to express your concepts and ideas, regardless of how outlandish they may be because I have faith that if you keep trying, you'll eventually hit it big. If you have the wherewithal and the wit, you can do anything." (Mr. S. – Manufacturing)

299.   "Don't get talked out of a good idea. Get away from the conventional wisdom. Don't join the crowd." (Mr. D. – Financial Services)

387.   "The greatest contribution that a leader can give any employee is the openness to think and be creative without the fear of making a mistake. We've all made mistakes, and we learn from those mistakes, and from mistakes comes our creativity." (Mr. J. – Manufacturing)

393.   "You must always encourage innovation. The world is an ever-changing place so your company needs to change with it. Look for ways to set yourself apart. Always try to put yourself in a position for success in the long term. Do this by staying in the know and using all the data available to you. You should always encourage creativity. I need not fear change or new things because those things can bring about the best products. Stay in front of your competition by understanding the past and being able to look into the future better than them. Act in the present to position yourself so you will be better off five years from now than you are now. Don't be afraid to try different things." (Mr. L. – Consumer Products)

503.   "I think the best thing I can tell you is how important it is to be able to bring something new to the table. At [this firm], we've got a lot of old guys who have been working here for 30-plus years, and they've got this business figured out. What we don't have a lot of is fresh perspective and new ideas. We don't have a lot of people who think outside our box, and that's what we really need. I think that's what everybody needs, and that's probably what's going to

get you hired: the ability to see what they're not seeing, or to give them something to think about that they haven't considered before. That's the X-factor these days." (Mr. R. – Manufacturing)

571.   "If I were to give any advice, I think it would be to find ways to exercise the right side of your brain. Whether you get it from academia or outside academia, find exercises that promote creative methods of developing solutions. This is hugely important. Get more comfortable with the need to think about things from a more creative perspective." (Mr. G. – Manufacturing)

583.   "Most creative breakthroughs occur when your back is against the wall." (Mr. H. – Hospitality)

585.   "You don't create on your own. Focus your efforts on fostering the creativity around you." (Mr. V. – Consumer Services)

588.   "Find a way to make a difference. Follow the rules, but find a way to be creative." (Mr. R. – Utilities)

658.   "Approach each day with a new set of eyes to be available and open to listening to new ideas and thoughts. Go into each day seeing things as if you had never seen them before." (Mr. H. – Financial Services)

671.   "Look beyond the obvious. Think logically, but in a different way." (Mr. M. – Manufacturing)

DECISION-MAKING

So here is the science and art of life together in action: it is D.A.O.I.D. – data, analysis, others' points of view, intuition and imagination, data check. That is the five-stage process that strategic thinkers go through. Try it. The good news is that your decisions do not have to be perfect; nobody's ever have been or ever will be. Don't grip or squeeze things too tightly into analysis paralysis. Just take what you have, and work like crazy.

8. "Every day you are faced with tough and difficult decisions that will have a high effect on the company. The answer isn't always right there in front of you in a textbook. Most the time you have to go with your gut instinct to make a decision, and that decision may not always be right. There are a lot of questions you should ask yourself before making a decision, such as questions that involve how you will affect the environment or society, how you will affect employees or customers, or how you will affect the company as a whole. When choosing a staff to work around you, you need to choose people who are smart and can communicate well. That way when you are faced with a difficult decision you'll have several different inputs rather than just yours. You need to be a learner from all those people. You need to listen to their input and consider where they are coming from." (Mr. M. – Utilities)

14. "Be well aware of the fact that everything you do affects another person. I think that definitely is

something students need to learn. Decisions they make can have a considerable the impact on other people. If a you consider other people in your decision, you make better decisions." (Mr. D. – Energy, Mining & Materials)

15. "It is your job to make the best decision. To do that you need the help of other people. However, you cannot put the responsibility on their shoulders because it is your job to solve the problem; but you do need to ask them for assistance." (Mr. B. – Retailing)

71. "One of the most difficult aspects of strategic management is being able to make the correct decision quickly. A lot of times there is an overwhelming amount of information to process for each decision to be made. Experienced leaders are able to sort through this data and determine which information is relevant, and which is not. Young MBAs have a tendency to spend too much time looking at irrelevant information that will more than likely cloud judgment, in addition to delaying a decision. This process of 'data mining' is best learned through observation of an individual who has perfected such a feat over time." (Mr. T. – Hospitality)

90. "A strategic manager must actively listen, and include the right people in the decision-making process. Lastly, the strategic manager must have the facts in order to make good decisions." (Mr. V. – Manufacturing)

95. "There is no such thing as a 'right' decision. Naturally there are clearly right and wrong ethical and moral predicaments, but beyond that what makes a

decision 'right' is not the actual decision, but one's execution of that decision into a right one." (Mr. P. – Financial Services)

110. "An MBA must teach you how to take incomplete data and make a decision, which is similar to what you will experience in the real world." (Mr. M. – Manufacturing)

130. "It is not as simple as it appears in books or cases. There are always a lot of complicating factors. Case studies are good to look at, but at the time decisions are made they seem like good ones, and then information changes. Hindsight is 100% accurate. You can always look back and know what you should have done, but when you are actually facing it decisions are not that simple." (Mr. N. – Financial Services)

135. "In their simplest form, management and leadership revolve around making choices. Since no organization can do all it wants to do, leaders must make choices about what they will and will not do. As a leader, your job is to make sure that the processes and systems are in place to help make those decisions. My approach begins with developing clarity around mission, vision, and core values. I believe that without a clear direction, no organization can be successful. However, just having a clear vision is not enough. A management system must be in place that translates that vision into the daily activities of the organization." (Dr. H. – Business Services)

146. "I believe that people make bad decisions because of a lack of objectivity. Therefore, I recommend that MBAs attempt to be as objective as

possible. Making decisions takes a disciplined thought process, while many MBAs want to simply fly by the seat of their pants. An MBA graduate needs to put all the facts on the table, and then make a decision from looking at all the data. However, I would warn that just because you have a lot of data does not mean that it is the right data. An MBA will need to objectively see if the data can help in the decision process." (Mr. G. – Food & Agriculture)

162.   "Be decisive but not clinical in decision making. It's not always a cut and dried path." (Mr. T. – Hospitality)

167.   "Do not make hasty decisions based on sheer whim. Even though I firmly believe that much of strategic management is based on intuition, if possible, you should really take the time to think about a problem or a proposition to make sure that all the details are worked out. As in life, if it sounds too good to be true, it probably is. When you need something good to happen, you should not jump at any opportunity that presents itself because it might not be the best thing for your company. Lastly, it is very important to know and trust your own head and your own heart for making strategic decisions. If you cannot trust your own knowledge and instinct, good decision making will be very difficult if not impossible." (Ms. S. – Business Services)

212.   "Avoid 'analysis paralysis.' That's a youthful phenomenon in which someone who lacks a lot of experience feels they need to know all aspects and factors surrounding a decision. What this means is that you can get so invested in looking for those factors that

you never get any closer to making a decision. To deal with this behavior, try to develop a judgment level. Having this level of judgment or 'gut instinct' allows you to move on with a decision with a limited amount of information. Once you have made a decision based on limited information, you must be willing to reassess the results of that decision as the implementation unfolds. If new information presents itself that shows you should revise your decision, then by all means do so. It is much more important to make a decision and move forward than to be mired in the decision-making process wasting time." (Mr. C. – Healthcare)

229.   "Be decisive. 'Ready, aim, shoot' is far better than 'Ready, aim, aim, aim...'" (Mr. T. – Consumer Products)

287.   "I do think that critical thinking skills are important to gain awareness of how to think through the potential ramifications of making a certain decision. The ability to understand the three things that are most likely to go wrong in a certain strategy, and being able to try to avoid those undesirable outcomes and prepare for them before they occur. I think it is so important that our management team has the ability to communicate effectively and understand that you have to make decisions even without all the information, plus the need to do so at a certain pace." (Mr. G. – Manufacturing)

346.   "You have to stand out and be unique. You have to be your own person and decide what works for you. I hear 600 opinions a day and they are all different, so you have to figure out things that will

work under a variety of conditions. There isn't a lot of black and white." (Mr. D. – Financial Services)

347. "The process of strategic management is not static; it is constantly on the move. An important factor is to find ways to involve enough of the organization in the decision making process. This will help you put the strategic vision together and be committed to executing a particular project." (Mr. F. – Construction)

353. "You should be able to rely on your upper management to assist you in decision-making processes. Attempting to make all decisions by yourself is a recipe for failure. And making sure those people are brighter than you will allow yourself to trust their decisions. Implementing a chain of command is very important to the operations of business." (Mr. K. – Consumer Services)

379. "I can tell you that the application of the principles that are taught to you, the success gained from those teachings, has to be applied in a loose form to any given situation. There is no black or white. You have to incorporate a lot of different experiences and teachings in order to reach a successful conclusion. It's a very difficult recipe to follow, and it changes from time to time." (Mr. O. – Information Technology)

381. "The stuff you learn in books and the things that you learn in school and classes are fundamental to understanding the strategy and management of organizations. I think when you get into doing it from a CEO level it is really about all the unknowns and the multi-faceted things that are coming to you, and how you take all that information that you learned from the

books and apply it to all the things that are being thrown at you to come out with a direction or a decision. That is what I do and what I think most CEOs do – to take that experience, which can be academic or on the job, and apply it to come up with an answer that is mostly right. If you do that, you are going to be successful. If not, you have to figure out if you can learn to do that. Getting a degree is interesting, but applying what you've learned is what it comes down to in order to be successful. You have to start out with the great benefit of learning it all, and then figure out how to apply it and adjust as you go, knowing full well that whatever you learn might have been time-stamped. What you learn in an MBA program is interesting and should be retained. How you learned it and how you will apply it is probably the more important question." (Mr. T. – Information Technology)

404. "Most of the time you are facing a choice that you do not know the answer to. Years later you find out whether you were right or wrong. If you were wrong, what are you going to do to right that wrong?" (Mr. E. – Entertainment & Media)

441. "In order to be successful you can't use excuses or cop-outs. You must take responsibility for the decisions you make no matter the outcome." (Mr. B. – Energy, Mining & Materials)

447. "I believe that the most successful people are the ones that make data-driven decisions, not gut reactions. Gut reactions can be way off. How I feel about something can be dangerous." (Mr. S. – Healthcare)

469.   "You are successful because of a few really big decisions. You've probably heard that you really only have what, maybe seven, major decisions in life. You know, who you marry, where you go to school... those. Well, it's that way in business too. People who are really amazing, there is lots of chance to that. Timing – a lot of things make a difference. You find what you like and you are good at it, but really, there is some luck. One decision, it can have a really dramatic effect. Lots of people pass up opportunities. The really key thing is that you have to recognize the opportunity, but a lot of people don't. They don't see it; they don't know what it is. They miss it, or just let it go. You have to be able to take risk. Entrepreneurs are successful because of the same characteristics. They find opportunities, and they have to take some risks. And those big decisions, that is what is going to make you successful. So you really have a few major decisions that direct everything." (Mr. C. – Business Services)

473.   "Ultimately, you have to make the decision and live with the decision. When you're the CEO you are completely alone. You can't go complain or whine or worry to the people you work with, and you can't bring it home to your family either. Ultimately, you're responsible for all decisions regarding the company. If you make a mistake, it's your fault. When you make the right decision, you have to make others feel like they've made the right decisions because you're responsible for inspiring them." (Mr. F. – Manufacturing)

670.   "You've got to know your numbers, no getting around that. You've got to know them better than

your boss does. Numbers are clear and unquestionable items of authority. If you are an expert with them, you can become unquestionable. It is an invaluable skill to gain the respect and credibility of your superiors. You have to always talk empirically about the business. This will give weight and relevance to your arguments and prompt others to listen to you." (Mr. R. – Entertainment & Media)

ETHICS AND INTEGRITY

Because everything you do impacts others, you need to consider ethics in all that you do. In everything. And because you have multiple, diverse parties depending on you, and their needs and values differ, you must be very clear about establishing and living by a solid system of values and priorities. What matters most? Why? What matters little? Why? Be the rock.

12.   "A good leader does not let their goals or beliefs be manipulated by others. Never compromise your principles. If you have to be attending to maintaining the respect of your employees, it is unlikely that you have it." (Mr. T. – Construction)

16.   "Managers will have thousands of opportunities to benefit from making an unethical decision, but don't do it." (Mr. T. – Business Services)

21.   "Ask yourself how much is your character worth? Standing for moral and ethical principles will bring you a great deal of grief. This is because of the rapid declining values of the business world. However, you will need to decide on which values mean the most to you and pick your fights accordingly. You will feel pressure, but by keeping high standards and moral integrity you can shape the environment and not need to fear doing wrong." (Mr. I. – Business Services)

22.   "Be honest, and do everything to the best of your ability. My father and his grandfather instilled honesty in me at an early age. From my experience,

you get in more trouble if you mess up and you aren't honest about it than if you are at fault and come clean. I believe that honesty is something that all managers, as well as their subordinates, must possess, or they will fall into a trap later in life that will catch up with them. Too often there is an 'any-means-possible' attitude about acquiring success in the business world. Be ambitious and driven, but you don't have to sacrifice honesty for success." (Mr. H. – Healthcare)

24.   "So many times, people get so caught up in their work that they lose perspective of what is most important in life. True personal fulfillment can only be obtained if one is morally upright and ethical when succeeding." (Mr. H. – Real Estate)

26.   "Be yourself, yet be honest and hold to your integrity. Throughout my career I have seen so many cases of how bad integrity in top management can turn a well-established company into a disaster." (Mr. D. – Financial Services)

47.   "Recognize the value of surrounding yourself with good people. The people that you surround yourself with should have integrity and be willing to work hard. I cannot emphasize enough the importance of working for a company that supports your individual values. If your company's priorities clash with your own, you will not be satisfied with the decisions made by the company. And if you truly are an individual with integrity, you will not be happy in a workplace with different values." (Mr. N. – Food & Agriculture)

80.   "Maintain integrity at all costs." (Mr. L. – Business Services)

112.   "Your credentials are less important than your character, commitment and competencies, and character is the most important. We can recall numerous CEOs collapsing due to character flaws, so I urge you to guard your integrity as you would your life. Never say anything, or write anything, or put anything in an e-mail that you wouldn't want on the front page of the newspaper." (Mr. D. – Business Services)

124.   "It is easy for people to act ethically in business in an environment like we have here. This is because the company will support its employees if they have acted ethically, and will immediately fire any employee who cannot be trusted. If a person builds an ethical reputation, it will spread and customers will return again and again. As long as you have a passion for your business and you act ethically, you will have better experiences and build a good reputation." (Mr. K. – Retailing)

141.   "In terms of ethics, a historical rule that our company has always functioned under is the golden rule: treat others the way you would like to be treated if the roles were reversed. That has served me very well for a very long time period. And it does not require writing a huge numbers of internal manuals and protocols and so forth where you tell people in writing that you're supposed to treat other person the way you'd like to be treated if the roles were reversed." (Mr. H. – Energy, Mining & Materials)

153. "It is important to always be up front and honest about any mistakes or bad news. Don't ever be devious." (Mr. L. – Healthcare)

154. "The key thing understand is that at the core of management or leadership should be a basic foundation of honesty and integrity. Upon that base you can balance the daily demands that are put on you. If you build this platform to work from, you will be able to live a life, and manage a company, that reflects everything you want to be. Those who we often view as the greatest leaders and managers throughout history are people who have conquered the vices and inconsistencies in their life. Whether it's ego, drinking, money or anything else, you must not let these things lead you off the path to success." (Mr. H. – Conglomerate)

177. "You have to be an evaluator of integrity so that as you are working in an organization and you are working for people, you have got to be able to feel as though you are working for people who have a high level of integrity and credibility. Otherwise you should not be there; it is not an organization you want to try to work your way up into." (Mr. C. – Financial Services)

186. "Run your business transparently; make it part of your mission statement. I must stress the importance of conducting business ethically. From my experience, an inability to do so will certainly lead to failure in the long run. Leaders who define and clearly communicate a vision, strategy, and direction for the organization provide certain guidance toward conducting

transparent business operations." (Mr. Y. – Consumer Services)

187.   "Just telling someone to do the right thing is a very open ended statement that is completely susceptible to interpretation. You must definitely clarify what the right thing is in a world where values are not necessarily clear. Establishing direction makes it easier to ensure that the company is following an ethical path. Nobody wants to go to jail." (Mr. S. – Entertainment & Media)

192.   "No matter what an individual does, they must operate with integrity. Accountability starts at the top; you cannot hold anyone to a higher ethical standard than you hold yourself. Although in this day and age the business world is closely regulated with legislative attempts to ensure integrity, nothing will be as successful as what comes from within you as the leader of your firm." (Mr. C. – Energy, Mining & Materials)

222.   "The most important thing you can do to have a great career is to find an organization that has very strong moral and ethical values. That's not to say that you might not have to just take a job, because we all are going to at some point, just have to take a job. However, it is important to search out a career path with a company that's ethically right for you. Remember, the quick buck is not always the best buck." (Mr. M. – Retailing)

229.   "Be honest with others and with yourself. Your integrity is who you are and how people will relate to you for years to come. It only takes one misstep. Use good judgment by always thinking carefully before

speaking or acting. It only takes a few seconds to be aware of the consequences of what you're about to do, and that is time well-spent." (Mr. T. – Consumer Products)

236. "Your good name is a valuable asset; it is yours to develop and control. No one can bring harm to it unless you engage in behavior or make decisions that allow it to be compromised." (Mr. R. – Construction)

256. "Be sure to surround yourself with very sound people who share strong principles as you should. Acquire and follow the core values that a company has to offer." (Mr. G. – Construction)

259. "People may feel like they don't belong in an organization if they're starting to have conflicts with their own belief system. If a person committed to an institution didn't like what he or she saw, the best way is to get out as soon as possible. Because if you can't embrace the corporate culture, if you can't embrace the idea of that organization, then the best thing to do is to part company." (Mr. J. – Financial Services)

260. "If you manage your character well, your reputation will take care of itself." (Mr. W. – Financial Services)

263. "Always be committed to excellence by conducting yourself with integrity. Always remember the golden rule as well, you must respect others and you must never have double standards." (Ms. H. – Financial Services)

269.   "Absolutely stick to your ethics and do not ever waver from them. You will at one point or another, if not immediately, regret it if you deviate from your true values. An exercise might even be to do your own personal statement on what are your values and what is important to you. Your own personal mission statement, if you will." (Mr. S. – Manufacturing)

296.   "Along the way you get to know people, people get to know you. They form opinions of you and they call upon those opinions somewhere down the road." (Mr. H. – Financial Services)

297.   "Let people know moral and ethical things are important to you. Let them know how five years from now you will measure your success. We all want to hire 'go-getters,' but we want good citizens too." (Mr. R. – Hospitality)

300.   "I'm really concerned about how people coming up through the educational system can assume a better attitude in life toward being ethical. I had a guy here last fall who's an alumni relations person from Harvard Business School We spent quite a little while talking about that, and he sent me some information on some second year classes that students are taking on ethics. But you know, if your parents don't help you learn what's right from wrong, I don't see how you get there very well. If you're 20 or 22 and you have a faculty member standing in front of the class trying to explain to you why it's important that you be honest with yourself and with your coworkers and with your customers and suppliers, I don't see how that takes very well. Maybe it does. We had some classes, some cases, when I was at the B-school that really didn't

have an answer. They were, 'What do you do when you have to pay a bribe to a customer to get the business? What the hell's the answer there?' We and some people said, 'No question, you pay the bribe.' Others said, 'Of course not.' Instructors said, 'If you don't get the business, you go bankrupt. Well, what do you do?' So, I'm concerned about that because I see politicians without integrity standing in front of Congress and lying through their teeth. And I see businesspeople doing the same thing. So, I think it's really important that you stress to your coworkers and your organization you're leading that honesty and integrity is really, really important. You can lie to people, but it doesn't work very long. It comes back to bite you – especially with e-mails these days." (Mr. B. – Consumer Products)

304. "Be the kind of person that delivers the bad news first. Such honesty will earn someone more respect than anything" (Mr. S. – Construction)

333. "First impressions are carried everywhere you go. The most important thing to have is a strong moral compass. You must not give into the pressures of the workplace that encourage you to lie, misrepresent your product, or give bad advice. If you do any of these things, you will lose credibility. A person's background and a person's first impression follow them everywhere." (Mr. E. – Healthcare)

354. "Be true to yourself. Don't ever be a part of something that you aren't ethically comfortable with. Find a place you feel good, and dedicate yourself to it." (Mr. M. – Hospitality)

371. "Try to get your own code of ethics that you want to live by. Then you wake up in the morning and try to live by that same code of ethics every day. I've got that. I know that code of ethics, how I treat people and what I do. And it should become consistent so people will respect that. Always be honest. You can't lead a company and be cheating on your wife. It doesn't work that way. You've got to be either one way or the other. People have to respect you. You've also got to give back. People love a good guy. It just works out that way." (Mr. K. – Consumer Products)

382. "Don't get into too big of a hurry to react. People that hurry make mistakes. That all goes back to ethics and those scandals. You just have to do it the old fashion way, one block on top of the other." (Mr. F. – Conglomerate)

392. "Develop your values and beliefs, and stay committed to them. Know that they will evolve over time, but as long as they are sound and morally based, they will not lead you down a path from which you cannot recover." (Mr. H. – Energy, Mining & Materials)

395. "You should learn to rank and weigh your values and the company's values, and then decide which values are more important than others." (Mr. S. – Manufacturing)

398. "You have got to have a good moral compass. If you don't feel comfortable in a company, get out. If the corporate culture of a company doesn't match what you think is right, get out and go somewhere else." (Mr. R. – Consumer Products)

401. "Recently, I tried to tell people at the Department of Education that I don't think there is enough focus on ethics. You have probably had one business ethics class, and you probably found it dull. Teachers need to relate situations in these types of classes to real life situations where people must come to decision points – where they make a decision that goes one way, or make a decision that goes another way, and there are things impacted on both sides. Some of it is culturally based. Our culture has become very instantaneous. Everything is demanded on time. Therefore, what you have is that anything anybody wants, they think they can get it, and get it now. They think they are entitled to it, and the idea of 'paying your dues' seems like it has gone out of style." (Mr. M. – Energy, Mining & Materials)

409. "Make sure your personal values and those of the company are in alignment. If not, change companies." (Mr. D. – Transportation)

426. "One must go back to your core values. These values can come from your religion or your family. In 'the fog of business' we have to look to our character and training. These core values will guide you when making strategic decisions." (Mr. C. – Energy, Mining & Materials)

448. "Never lose your moral and ethical compass to fall back on what you know is right and wrong. If you have to make a decision that lies within a gray area, do not rush the decision. Sit back; think, and get advice from other leaders." (Mr. L. – Consumer Services)

454. "No matter what, happiness should always come first. When it comes to finding the perfect job, you have to make sure that the atmosphere, working conditions, and the company's corporate culture all agree with what you stand for as an individual. If a company does not mold to your morals and values, there will be conflict later on." (Mr. W. – Financial Services)

482. "Have a set of core values. I think that having core values helps you to focus on the right strategies and to manage them well. Always be ethical and do the right thing every day. Even though you're going to make mistakes, try to do the right thing." (Mr. E. – Manufacturing)

551. "Remember always be true to yourself. Remember, if it is moral, legal, and ethical I am going to give it a shot. But if it doesn't touch any of those three – if any of those is left out – it is off the table. And then you do not have to worry about a lot of problems. People will admire you for that. They will believe that this guy is honest; this guy is going to do what is right, what is fair. He is going to be relentless; he is going to expect the best, but he is going to be fair and consistent about it. I think if you can live with that, then you have lots of opportunity going down the road. Harry Truman once said if you tell the truth you never have to remember what you said. There is so much truth to that. Just play it straight. Those kind of things come back around to pay dividends for you." (Mr. R. – Financial Services)

565.   "Treat people the way you want to be treated. If you do that, you will find opportunities come to you." (Mr. S. – Food & Agriculture)

662.   "Never forget what you have promised." (Dr. K. – Healthcare)

EXPERIENCE AND EDUCATION

Beware the trap of either-or thinking. Most things that matter work best to the degree that we approach them in terms of "both-and." That is paradoxical logic. So in that way consider your own portfolio of knowledge and/or skills. Experience "or" education? Which do you need more of to balance this vital paradox? to make yourself well-rounded?

37.   "Lifetime learning is a critical success factor for individuals, and that is what most MBAs do not understand. Once you get integrated into the company and the company culture, then you can use your education and all the tools you learned in school to benefit the company. That is when you can make a difference." (Mr. P. – Manufacturing)

45.   "What many MBAs are lacking is the execution skills which must be learned in a real world environment. You have to make mistakes and learn and grow from the experience. The gist is that an MBA might give you an education in the fundamentals of business, but experience in the field gives you the judgment and skills necessary to execute the chosen strategy successfully." (Mr. T. – Hospitality)

57.   "Your learning is not over. Do not throw away your notes and your text books. Always look for opportunities to learn from your experiences, your peers, your subordinates, and your bosses. Do not be surprised how many of the theories you talked about you actually get to put in to practice. Topics you only

spoke of briefly may become everyday occurrences for you. Putting theory into practice takes time and experience, so the best method for a new manager is to be a good listener, and to take advantage of the minds and experience around you." (Mr. D. – Manufacturing)

58.   "I don't like seeing some MBAs come out and act so rigid with all of the things they learned in their textbooks. Students need to take what's in the textbook and apply it to everyday life, and not hold the textbook as 'the gospel.' The world is changing so rapidly that if a textbook was written last year, it's already out of date. So it is vitally important to keep up with current world events and business news." (Mr. V. – Business Services)

61.   "Approach management as a practical experience as opposed to something from a book. Books are good for learning the basics, but not everything you read is true. Top managers need to think beyond books." (Mr. B. – Information Technology)

75.   "What you need to understand about strategic management is that it takes experience and savvy to deal with circumstances and situations, that you gain experience in dealing with people, and that being predictably successful in different kinds of roles does not come innately. It's gained through experience." (Mr. D. – Entertainment & Media)

87.   "Formal education is great, but it only provides the platform to begin with. Formal education puts you in the position to learn and understand what you are

trying to accomplish. Having a degree does not mean that you know business. Knowing business comes from actually working in it. Time in the trenches is worth more than a world of education. Students leave college with an ideal picture of how to manage business, but textbook prescriptions do not always work." (Mr. K. – Manufacturing)

90. "Most academic theories, when applied to our business, create negative results. Not that academics aren't bright, but they lack important context." (Mr. V. – Manufacturing)

91. "You need to learn how to fill the gap between the tools that we have learned and the real world. There are some things one cannot learn from books or professors; these are what I call the 'gaps.' The challenge for business schools is to try to fill these gaps quickly by adjusting their curricula to ongoing rapid changes in the business environment." (Mr. T. – Hospitality)

124. "The nature of a person's education should depend on their ultimate career goals. A mechanic for example, should master the techniques of repairing vehicles. A businessperson, however, should have a broad education and be open minded." (Mr. K. – Retailing)

143. "Everything in the real working environment initially seems different from school. But when you look back on what you learned in management classes, all of the theories seem to pretty much line up. You can't expect to jump in the business world and follow

a textbook; but looking back, the theories do make sense." (Mr. L. – Manufacturing)

178. "You have already learned many management theories in class, and this professional knowledge will be helpful when you become a manager or CEO in the future. What you need to do is to relate what you have learned in class to the real business world. Maybe it will be a little bit difficult at the beginning, but you will gain more useful experience when you try to do that." (Mr. R. – Manufacturing)

182. "Experience is the premium quality anyone can possess with regards to management. Education is important, and in many cases a necessity as well, but experience trumps all things. Generally, MBAs are a dime a dozen." (Mr. J. – Healthcare)

189. "Continue to educate yourself. Refer back to teachings from your management classes, and keep reading *The Wall Street Journal.* I would stress the importance of always being on top of the news in order to educate yourself. Always go back to your textbooks when the principles of management actually apply to real life situations. I recall taking an Organizational Behavior class and not really understanding what the instructor was talking about. However, once I got out into the real world and was mature enough to go through certain situations, the management principles I had learned started to make much more sense." (Mr. G. – Construction)

278. "I feel there is a difference between theoretical knowledge and practical life. My advice to you is to

keep your mind open and learn new things from experience." (Mr. P. – Manufacturing)

279. "You want to take what you learn and use it. Hopefully that will make you more valuable to your employer, and also give you opportunity to do things which you wouldn't have otherwise been able to do absent that knowledge and absent that confidence that you get in having been exposed to your classwork and relationships developed with your classmates. So, that's the way I think your education should be used. It shouldn't be used as 'I got my MBA and now I am worth a million dollars, and you should pay me that or I am going to go somewhere else.' I think that has been an unfortunate byproduct of everyone getting an MBA. If you have an opportunity to improve your financial well-being, you should do it, but don't assume that since you got your MBA you are worth a lot more money. It's not a key; it's a tool so that you can be better with your 'hammers and screwdrivers' than the average Joe. But an MBA is not a free pass to Go." (Mr. W. – Healthcare)

280. "As an MBA, you have shown your drive and commitment to knowledge. That is great and an excellent trait. But never forget though that a large majority of the theory is much less relevant than you think. Experience is always going to be the true classroom." (Mr. S. – Information Technology)

284. "Realize that your MBA doesn't entitle you to anything. People have come to me and said, 'But I have an MBA.' Good for you. I think a MBA gives you a set of tools that should allow you to demonstrate a capability beyond someone else. It's that, a

demonstration; it's not an entitlement. With your MBA you have to focus on business acumen and don't lose face on that. Your tendency when you get into a job will to be pulled a certain way. Your MBA should teach you to always think broader and develop that business acumen as broadly as you can. Stay current. That is what a MBA will do for you. It will give you that orientation and that mindset to think broader. I love a technical background with a MBA. I think it is a good to have a technical base with a broad business background. The combination is really strong. That should allow you when you problem solve and get exposure to different things to apply a little different logic to what needs to be done." (Mr. R. – Manufacturing)

289.   "One thing, as a word of wisdom, is don't believe the books. Have you ever heard the expression 'Those who can, do. Those who can't, teach. Those who can't teach, teach teachers'? Every time I read these books I think, 'If you're so smart, why aren't you doing it?' Be very nervous of those books. Be very nervous of the science of business. I studied physics and I am biased because of being a physicist. Business is common sense. There is no hard math in business. There is nothing difficult. It's common sense and people. Things like the Five Forces are right not because they are clever and brilliant, but because they are simple. You look at it and say, 'Well I could have told you that. I couldn't have drawn such a nice diagram, but I could have told you that.' It's when you see stuff and think, 'Yeah, that's a nice illustration of something I already knew.' You kind of know it's right, but it's nice because it makes you feel like it makes sure you have thought of everything every time you think

about it. If you read 'From Good to Great' for example, the way they found the companies that were the best and so on, the math and the logic is just nonsense. There is a very famous book by Tom Peters called 'In Search of Excellence' about the great companies like IBM and others. Literally a couple of years after he wrote it a bunch of them were in big trouble. This idea that you can find perfect companies and copy them and you'll be perfect is just not true. It's just common sense and people. Circuit City was one of the 'Good to Great' companies and they are no longer in business. But they were good, for a while. Everybody is good, for a while. There are companies that Jim Collins calls out as being great with all of these humble leaders. There is a lot of nonsense written. Gary Hammel wrote a book, but there is a lot of nonsense written. You have to be careful of it. Just be pragmatic. Be pragmatic and have common sense because it is just common sense and people." (Mr. S. – Consumer Products)

291.   "The number one thing that will teach more lessons than any educational institution is adversity. You may learn the fundamentals and scientific process in school, but it is all tied together throughout work experience. If it is tied together in an adverse work experience, one can walk away with more lessons that will help them prepare for the future. I would never wish adverse working conditions on anyone, but it is a Darwinistic environment that molds survivors into galvanized business professionals." (Mr. B. – Manufacturing)

292.   "With an MBA, employers look for you to be self-motivated and a quicker learner. Employers look at the MBA degree as teaching students to think outside

of the box and be able to handle themselves in any corporate setting. There will be many more opportunities as an MBA, but there will also be many more expectations." (Mr. S. – Business Services)

310. "Having an MBA is great, but practical experience is the best teacher that you can ever have. Getting beat up and learning the lesson that you made a bad decision, and knowing that just because you have a MBA does not mean that you have all the answers. It requires taking information and applying it in an appropriate fashion to whatever you're dealing with in the work environment, whatever environment that may be. People have gone right into a master's program right out of college. That was the way it used to be done. They thought that they would make a gazillion dollars having that MBA, like it was a golden ticket. It can be helpful, but I think from what I am hearing and reading that a lot of business schools like the fact that somebody has been working for a year or two. It is a tough world now." (Mr. P. – Financial Services)

311. "Understand that what you have learned is just a step in your journey. You may understand the theories, but an MBA is just a tool in being able to offer value to a customer. I think too many MBAs expect that 'Now that I have an MBA, I am a lot smarter than a guy who doesn't have one, and hence should be treated differently.' It is still going to come down to how you utilize what you have been taught. I have seen some MBAs fail because they have an expectation that those letters behind their names will open lots of doors for them. Well, they absolutely will open doors, but once you walk in that door, you've still got to

prove yourself. Just remember that what you have learned is only the first step; applying it is more important." (Mr. G. – Business Services)

313.   "An MBA is a great title, but all it means is that you should be well-rounded, like any other degree. I never look at where people went to school. You have something everyone else has; you are on the same playing field. You have the same entrée that someone else already has. Why did you get your MBA? You have to use it to exceed expectations. That degree doesn't give you the job. I'm a real-life CEO, but I started with nothing. Nothing was beneath me. I was a janitor cleaning buildings because I couldn't afford not to. An MBA degree means nothing is beneath you; the degree doesn't make you successful. I look for employees that are 'bumblebees.' Theoretically, bumblebees should not be able to fly, but they do. A bumblebee exceeds expectations. So should you." (Mr. T. – Conglomerate)

317.   "In the real world there are many styles of managing your business. Two of the most important are street sense and gut reactions. Sometimes you just have to manage by those two philosophies, not by the book." (Mr. P. – Consumer Services)

319.   "Education has become more of a commodity and less of an advantage. A degree is important, but graduate school can't replace the importance of real world experience." (Mr. W. – Transportation)

329.   "The greatest teacher is not what is in a book, but experience. As you grow as a leader, you need to balance your experience with continuing education and the latest academic thinking. Learn from your

current leaders. Learn what they do well, but equally important, learn what not to do." (Mr. B. – Retailing)

370. "What I learned I learned by the seat of my pants and the school of hard knocks. Don't be afraid to set the textbooks aside and learn from experience. It is a very effective teacher." (Ms. I. – Food & Agriculture)

373. "There is no set way of doing business or managing. Through experience you learn to adapt to your job as you strike a balance between your own personality and the environment and culture of the organization. Classroom learning helps provide good management fundamentals, but more in-depth management skills can only be achieved through work experience." (Mr. M. – Financial Services)

379. "An MBA is only a ticket to go to the game, but it's not a ticket to put you on the field and play. In other words, it puts you in the game and gives you the opportunity, but it doesn't guarantee your success." (Mr. O. – Information Technology)

392. "Students need to understand that strategic management isn't something that can strictly be taught. Experience over time is the key development tool for transforming a reasonably bright and educated person into someone that can formulate and implement strategic activities. The process isn't always linear." (Mr. H. – Energy, Mining & Materials)

393. "Don't go to MBA school just to pass the time without any real world experience." (Mr. L. – Consumer Products)

397. "You should learn all you can in college and enjoy your time there. College is the only place where you can learn a certain style of thought that is priceless. You can learn business smarts from experience, but a college education is invaluable. College kids are so important in our business because they are so fresh on the information that we old people have forgotten." (Mr. G. – Financial Services)

399. "Students need to understand that strategic management is really, really, really complicated. If anybody thinks that they can lay it all out in a textbook and read everything they need to know, then they are wrong. It takes years of experience and actively working in it to understand it. I have never understood how consultants can send students that are just right out of school to provide solutions for a well-established company. If you have not experienced it, how can you recommend solutions? A high IQ and GPA cannot take the place of real world experience. People need to get experience before they can offer advice. I don't think I am being naïve; I know that people can have new ideas that we couldn't see from inside the organization. However, I would generally ask the help of an industry specialist and let that be the end of the line. Like I said, experience is key. Managing a firm is much too complex to understand without the experience." (Mr. F. – Manufacturing)

399. "I don't have a lot of respect for those who gloat about or have multiple, high-level degrees and no experience to back it up. Much of what you learn in school will have little day-to-day applicability in your job. I would not look at an applicant any more who has multiple high degrees than one traditional

candidate for a job. I have seen many cases where higher education has failed to prepare students for the real world. One thing I will say for education is that accounting is incredibly important in business, as well as simple and general math skills. Almost every major business decision involves a number." (Mr. F. – Manufacturing)

412. "You have to earn your seat at the table. You can get a Harvard MBA, then go and get a Dartmouth MBA, then get a Yale MBA, and you'll still lack credible experience, and people will not take you as seriously. Go get real work experience. Then I'll listen to you, but not until then." (Mr. R. – Business Services)

432. "The base of what you learn is in the book, but when you hit the real world you need experience – on the job training – and you need to be adaptable. Don't use the textbook. Learn the industry as much as you can." (Mr. W. – Financial Services)

486. "Getting back to the value that I saw in my MBA – don't take this wrong – I actually valued my MBA more than I would have if I went from college to MBA because I had about six years of business experience. Translating strategic theory into reality is hard. Once MBAs get on the ground and get into a company it's no longer about what was in the strategy book but the real life situation that you are involved in. I doubt that any MBA would ever find any answer to the strategy question in any book that they read. What the book teaches you to do is to think correctly." (Mr. L. – Information Technology)

495. "You must understand that you lack the experience that most companies are looking for. Regardless of all your education and energy, you just don't have it, and there is no way to gain that experience without working for a while. It stinks and it is unfair, but that's just the way it is. So you have to come up with creative ways to set yourself apart from everyone else. But once you obtain some experience you will be surprised with the opportunities that will present themselves." (Mr. S. – Information Technology)

496. "Education is very important. When you leave school, your learning is just starting. You must keep up with seminars and educational opportunities. Learn from every single person you interact with. Coming out of school in a hurry or thinking that you know everything won't get you anywhere." (Mr. B. – Healthcare)

536. "The main advice that I have would be to gain all of the real world experience that you can. These kinds of experiences only come from talking to people in entry-level positions, middle management, and then on up the ladder. It is one thing to understand the why's of running a corporation, but it's a totally different ballgame to understand the how's. Successful people know both." (Mr. O. – Transportation)

544. "Ignore a lot of what you learned from your education because you will have to adapt and learn new things that may even be the opposite of what you were taught." (Mr. F. – Financial Services)

FEEL AND INTUITION

Empirical data and rigorous analysis are the rock upon which success is built. Then soft skills are what set you apart – above and beyond. They are the skills that ultimately guide us in things of humanity and life for which there are no measures or formulas. And as your career progresses, these intangibles will be the heart and soul of your greatest contributions.

19. "Trust your instincts. Often, when crucial decisions need to be made we spend way too much time trying to convince ourselves of something other than what our gut instinct told us first. We end up talking ourselves out of it, or let someone else talk us out of our first thought, which is usually the best decision." (Mr. J. – Business Services)

33. "It takes years of hands-on experience through many trials and errors that a person develops understanding, or intuition; so don't be afraid to take risks." (Mr. G. – Financial Services)

40. "You need to be prepared to make decisions with data that may not contain all the answers needed to make a decision. This is the 'gut' or 'intuition' part of strategic management. Look beyond the obvious." (Mr. B. – Manufacturing)

72. "The main thing is to know how to filter which information is good information and which people to trust is key. And at the end, use your gut feeling to make the final decision. This requires that you have

good people around you who will give you the right information. In the case that information is conflicting and not enough for you to make a decision, go to an outside consulting agency and get their input also. But even after that, once again, go with your gut feeling to make the decision. Gain both experience and knowledge so that you can follow your personal instincts and morals." (Mr. D. – Construction)

115. "Don't ever think you know everything; always exhaust all resources before you make a decision. Every company must be data driven, but don't forget to come out and let your feelings and gut instinct help you make decisions." (Mr. W. – Manufacturing)

367. "You really don't understand strategic management until you've done it. You can't learn strategic management from a book. You can learn the science of management from school, but you must learn the art of strategic management by practicing it. In management there is a significant amount of 'feel' required. A sort of 'sixth sense' that tells you how to react in situations that don't follow textbook logic or seem obvious." (Dr. T. – Information Technology)

457. "You never know nearly as much as you think you do. You'll be surprised at how often things come into play and you don't even know they are coming into play. You'll meet people who intuitively make the right decision. They understand and feel the tenets of business; they sense the core realities. It's a combination of philosophy and judgment that lead you to take this action over another action. In some ways you will know more than people you'll be

working with, but in other ways you've got a lot to learn still." (Mr. N. – Entertainment & Media)

577.   "The final advice I can give that I hope you can take and use is to be fearless in your career, but at the same time trust your gut instinct. Always know that you are the person who knows you best, and you know what you can and can't do in a situation. Follow your gut, and don't be afraid to go down a path no one has ever gone down before." (Mr. A. – Business Services)

579.   "Don't ever listen to someone who tells you your idea is full of hot air when your gut is telling you, 'There is a possibility for success here.'"   (Mr. W. – Information Technology)

582.   "Always remain inquisitive, open-minded and flexible. When dealing with uncertainty, follow your heart and your gut and always remain courageous. When you open a door and the room is totally black, you must have faith to take the first step." (Mr. R. – Healthcare)

654.   "Managing strategically calls for under-standing, insight and intuitive feel in picking up threads and reading between the lines." (Mr. P. – Construction)

FOCUS

A two-edged sword here: a laser beam can cut through steel, heal the body, penetrate the black void of space. And it can utterly destroy. All elite performance requires undivided focus. Closely observe elite performers in any field; they are all business. There is no sense of "whatever" in their disciplines. Yet along with this awe-inspiring power comes the potential for narrow-mindedness, rigid inflexibility, and insensitivity. It's in your hands.

9.   "You need to find out what you're good at and stay focused on it. Then you can build on what comes out of that, and the company will prosper. It's a big mistake to look around and try to do too many things when you could instead focus on your core areas of expertise." (Mr. B. – Business Services)

23.   "The toughest thing is learning how to identify what is important and what isn't so you know where to focus your efforts with your limited time." (Mr. P. – Business Services)

28.   "You should not worry about the score too much. Instead, it's more important to know where the momentum is heading. Worry about the things that you can affect. Focus on driving the independent variables, not the dependent ones." (Mr. V. – Consumer Products)

168.   "Never lose sight of your particular mission. Always be aware of why your business exists and how

it got there. Almost every business sector is very specific and unique from another, so you need to remember why you are doing what you do. You have to maintain that focus to serve your market better. If you lose focus, you will not be able to effectively manage, and you will be lost in what you are trying to do." (Mr. G. – Healthcare)

281.   "Have peripheral vision and be alert, but if you focus on doing a good job at where you are, you will find that the opportunities will come to you. Keep it simple. My favorite quote from Leonardo Da Vinci was 'Simplicity is the ultimate sophistication.' In this day and age, we try to make things more complicated than they really are, particularly with access to information. Don't make things complicated." (Mr. S. – Consumer Products)

362.   "Success is more about sustained, disciplined focus than brilliant strategy." (Mr. W. – Financial Services)

422.   "It's about painting a picture. It's about painting a picture. The picture becomes the road map. It's like driving down the road with no map. If you don't have a map, you will get lost. If you do you get off the path, you need that map to get you back on. Stay focused on what you want to accomplish." (Mr. T. – Financial Services)

427.   "Keep focused on the current job responsibility you have in order to become the best; that's what prepares you for the next opportunity – the ability to focus, get things done, break down problems, and find solutions." (Ms. S. – Retailing)

573. "I think there are too many generalists graduating from colleges. My suggestion would be to focus on one area and specialize in that." (Dr. H. – Food & Agriculture)

576. "That's pretty easy, it's focus and intensity. With focus, there are so many people and competitors that cannot focus on the task at hand; they're not good at it. So I've always been one to have a razor sharp focus on the task at hand. That's first and foremost. The second thing is intensity. People will pursue their work with a very ho-hum lack of intensity, so you can beat them if you are more intent on your work." (Mr. J. – Consumer Products)

HUMILITY

Humility here neither means nor implies self-doubt, low self-esteem, or weakness. It is the willingness to learn and the ability to be taught. It builds our powerful potential to change, grow and progress. It is the root of strength. Let go a little. Defending what we are hides us from what we can become. To the degree that you are concerned with getting respect, your insecurity is blocking your progress. Listen. Learn. Lead.

38.   "Nobody knows everything about strategic management, especially straight out of school. Too many MBAs come out of graduate school thinking they know everything about strategic management, or they discount what other more experienced managers have to say. You need to understand that not everything is black and white in the real world even though graduate school can make it look that way. Make strides to get along with everyone. I've seen too many MBAs come out of school thinking they know everything, creating friction between the green MBAs and weathered managers. You should strive to not burn bridges and to work on forming bonds and trust with other managers and co-workers. I feel that some MBAs have a natural arrogance to them out of graduate school; they really need to work on overcoming this." (Mr. C. – Business Services)

68.   "Do not get hung up with your own self-importance or you may be heading for a big disappointment. The reason is that you are coming out of school with theoretical stuff. You have to ask

Humility

questions like 'Why?' much more often than you are
used to. I do it all the time. So think less about your
self-importance. You are not a God-given expert in all
these things." (Dr. L. – Biotechnology)

80.   "Assume that you do not know it all, and that
you can learn something from anybody. Many people
feel that they can only learn from someone who is
smarter, but this is not true. What you need is a
fundamental humility – the belief that you can learn
from anyone." (Mr. L. – Business Services)

146.   "MBAs need to keep their ego separate from
their work. In fact, one of the reasons many MBAs fall
into traps is that they have so much pride in their plan
that they are not willing to reassess it when necessary.
Many MBAs often let their ego cause them to protect
bad decisions. Now, although I do believe in egoless
management; I have as big an ego as anyone. The key
to overcoming this is to keep the ego separate from
work. I have needed to suppress my ego over the years,
and not get in the way so that smarter people than
myself can make decisions that relate to their expertise.
This problem of ego is my number one answer as to
why intelligent, highly motivated executives make bad
decisions." (Mr. G. – Food & Agriculture)

191.   "To be an effective leader of any business, you
must be willing to not only flood yourself with
information on your company, but also be willing to
accept your shortcomings and ask for help." (Mr. D. –
Retailing)

222.   "One thing a lot of people don't think about is
the humbleness. The reason is people need to feel

113

important, and they need to feel like they are the key person to that organization. A leader must be humble enough to be able to make each employee feel this way. A leader must have confidence; however, confidence can result in arrogance, and arrogance doesn't make a good leader." (Mr. M. – Retailing)

226. "Early on if you're a manager in a company, be patient and don't try to come out of the gate and be the hot shot. I think you need to come in a little bit humble with the attitude that you want to learn. You know, that's why you have two ears and one mouth, because you're supposed to listen twice as much as you talk. You need to listen." (Mr. S. -- Entertainment & Media)

228. "Try to remember that the best strategists, especially in the business world, have controlled egos. Advice and good counsel can and do come from everywhere. Be open to it. Enjoy the journey." (Mr. S. – Entertainment & Media)

263. "You should always have self-confidence, but you are never to step over the line of being arrogant." (Ms. H. – Financial Services)

265. "One thing I found most important for me over the years is never getting full of yourself, remembering where you came from. Remember that you're going have good days and bad days. Remember, no matter how bad the day is it could always be worse. No matter how good the day is it could always be better. It comes back to humility combined with having that understanding." (Mr. G. – Healthcare)

293.   "Take your job very seriously, but don't take your title seriously." (Mr. G. – Financial Services)

299.   "Always respect the people around you." (Mr. D. – Financial Services)

300.   "Don't get a chip on your shoulder just because you have an MBA. I got mine from Harvard and I'm quite sure that there are people who got a Bellarmine, or a UK, or a U of L MBA that are much smarter than I am. But you'll have a bunch of other people who are ambitious, who kind of maybe don't know how to go, maybe have an overly generous opinion of themselves – you've probably encountered a few of those. Those people can be destruction for an organization." (Mr. B. – Consumer Products)

336.   "When I was 22 years old, one of my mentors pulled me into his office and told me that I must know nine words. If I remembered those nine words, I could do anything and would be a success. The words are, 'I am in trouble. I need your help please.' We are never good enough to solve every problem ourselves. There is always someone out there who could help us. We just have to know how to ask for that help and not be too proud to do so." (Mr. K. – Manufacturing)

339.   "Don't get hung up on building up your ego too much. Don't get so full of yourself. Don't start believing what people say about you." (Ms. H. – Financial Services)

343.   "In order to be effective at anything you attempt, you must remember that you have two ears and only one mouth. The people who you would want to be your mentors have a lot of experience and

advice to give you. Listen to it. Learn from their mistakes and build upon them. This will allow you to start off a step higher than they did. Choose your words carefully." (Mr. M. – Healthcare)

346. "I started out as a teller. I thought I was too smart to be a teller, and it kind of made me have a chip on my shoulder. I never thought I'd end up here as CEO though. I am so glad I went through that now though. Those girls down there can't come up here and shut the door like I can. They have to deal with whatever the customer or anyone else has to say. I've been there and realize that. It makes me respect everyone a little more because I've been in the same situation." (Mr. D. – Financial Services)

383. "I think there needs to be a certain amount of humility. We don't know it all. There is so much we have to get better at. We are not that good, and that starts with me. I'm always willing to be part of a culture that makes mistakes. I make mistakes; I try stuff. We make mistakes. We do everything 90% great because that is as good as you can get." (Mr. V. – Retailing)

393. "Short term success seems great, but it gives an inflated view of the company. Every CEO has to keep this in perspective. It is important to not get to cocky about any success of your business. Remember that there are lows and highs." (Mr. L. – Consumer Products)

424. "There are a lot of very smart people in college and universities, especially from the student's perspective. When a student graduates it does not

make them an expert; it just shows the employer that they are capable of learning. Do not enter your place of employment and think of yourself as an expert; always be teachable and willing to learn." (Mr. B. – Construction)

433.   "Maybe the most important lesson in any level of management is that we all have blind spots. No single person has all the answers. So we have to offer certainty for others so they can focus, but we also have to be willing to be uncertain for ourselves. Practice recognizing what others can teach you." (Ms. T. – Consumer Products)

443.   "Be humble. Just do it. It will pay unbelievable dividends. My dad would tell me, 'Don't have that five minutes of great pleasure telling someone off; he may end up being your boss or your customer. And you've lost that relationship for having your five minutes of 'fun.' Pick your fights, and there should be damn few of them. In management, if you find yourself arguing with people, then you're doing something wrong. When you go to a superior and you have an idea and you know it's a good idea, and they don't buy it, don't be tempted to do what a lot of young people do and act haughtily. Whenever I failed to sell an idea, I would blame myself. I didn't blame the customer or the employer or the investor. Instead, I would analyze the conversation and try to figure out where it went south. Then I would go back and try again. If you have a good idea, give it time; sell it slowly. Never believe your idea will completely come to fruition in one meeting." (Mr. R. – Transportation)

476. "Once in a position of making strategic decisions, MBAs will need to be eager to learn and not allow their ego to get in the way. Do not think that any degree qualifies you for a special position, or that you are better than anyone else." (Mr. D. – Manufacturing)

497. "Ask a lot of questions and learn from other people that have been around. I always thought my boss was wrong about what he told me to do and how he told me to do it. Later, I discovered he was right and I was wrong. Accept the fact that you may not always agree with your boss, but you ought to go ahead and do it. Give it time before you are overly critical about what the boss thinks is right or wrong. Be patient when criticizing, because like me, you might just find out one day that your boss was right all along, and you will then learn from your actions." (Mr. W. – Manufacturing)

554. "You need to be able to ask for and accept feedback from others. Don't be afraid to ask your boss and colleagues for advice on things you need to improve on over time. It will only help to make you stronger and better." (Mr. D. – Food & Agriculture)

LEADING PEOPLE

Everything you do in your work hinges on mastery of the principles in this chapter. Everyone influences others. Everyone is influenced by others. We are all connected. No title, rank or authority is required. Lead the way!

1. "No one wants to follow a person that does not follow through on promises or expectations. If a CEO says he is going to do something, it is in his best interest to deliver on those promises. Good strategic management does not center around oneself. A CEO brings the whole organization together to operate as one, but should not constantly flex his muscle, or micromanage the entire organization. That often yields negative results. If the CEO is practicing good management, he gives up personal control and influence but is rewarded with the creativity and passion that goes along with giving other managers some type of ownership of what is going on in the company." (Mr. N. – Entertainment & Media)

21. "Remember that you are dealing with people and through people to accomplish any given goal. You must be able to get people to buy in, and then sustain that drive to whatever end you seek. Leaders who use a dictatorial style will not last in their work. One must really listen to employees, staff and customers." (Mr. I. – Business Services)

30. "It starts with you, but doesn't end with you. Lead people to conclusions; don't enforce a mandate." (Mr. A. – Financial Services)

35.   "It is important to act like a leader rather than a manager. A leader challenges the process and inspires a new vision of the firm, while a manager is submerged in routines." (Mr. B. – Financial Services)

37.   "You need to be a good follower before you can become a good leader. Too many people come out of college and think they need to make all sorts of changes immediately to be effective, thinking that they know how to be the CEO right away.   Instead, you must enter the business and learn from all those within the company." (Mr. P. – Manufacturing)

61.   "A true leader must take responsibility not only for their own actions, but also the actions of their employees. A leader must help employees reach their maximum potential. A leader must have the ability to deal with multiple problems at the same time. They must find the right balance between doing the job versus delegating. And critically, a leader must devote their time to coaching and training others who have the potential and are aspiring to become managers someday." (Mr. B. – Information Technology)

63.   "I must emphasize the importance of taking a personal interest in those that you lead. As leaders, we should be concerned with what is going on in the lives of our employees. I recommend that you make special efforts to get to know your co-workers both in and outside the workplace.   By doing this, we are able to build the trust and respect that is essential to success in a management position." (Mr. G. – Transportation)

67.   "One of the lost arts in management is to avoid managing from the executive office without knowing

what is going on at the bottom floor. Direct customer and employee contact and input is vital and something many executives overlook or take for granted. Plans and initiatives that sound good in theory are not always realistic or practical once they reach the customer. In addition, associates have to believe in what the company is doing for successful execution. Providing them input opportunities enhances their 'buy in' of what your strategies are trying to accomplish." (Mr. T. – Financial Services)

69.   "It is easier to lead others if you do not have internal conflicts within yourself regarding who you actually are and who you portray yourself to be. This will allow for one to maintain their integrity and will allow others to believe in who is leading them." (Mr. D. – Financial Services)

70.   "The management-employee bond translates to a similar bond between employees and customers." (Mr. R. – Financial Services)

74.   "Don't forget that to be an excellent manager you should always be thinking about the people you work with. Not only your direct reports, but everyone you come in contact with. A truly excellent strategic manager is always motivating and leading people. A good strategic manager can motivate and lead those outside of their direct reports whether they are contractors working on a project, or employees within the company. MBAs need to remember that to be good strategic managers they should always be leading and inspiring others through their words or their actions." (Mr. D. – Healthcare)

77.　"People are the cornerstone of any business. And dealing with people is the most important task of a CEO. Understand that you need to have good people that you can trust beneath you. Then, make a concerted effort to understand how to interact with them. Be sure to show them that you are interested in the work they are doing and the quality with which they are doing it. An employee needs to see that their product is being used. Learning what makes people succeed and exceed expectations is everything." (Mr. R. – Financial Services)

86.　"MBAs are good the at the procedural and process side of running a business. But what I really need to see are more of the people skills – the much less tangible and more subjective side of handling individuals with tact. It's becoming a lost art. With more and more people getting MBAs, it's becoming harder and harder to find good leaders with an MBA on their resume." (Mr. T. – Manufacturing)

99.　"I cannot clap with one hand. I am limited by 24 hours, sleep, and the ability to reach people. You should understand that with better people, teamwork, and communication, you can much more effectively manage. This allows a good manager to multiply the results he or she could individually produce. You should understand that you will not have all the good ideas, but you should learn how to prioritize ideas submitted by other employees. People are always the answer to problems. These aren't necessarily the most educated or intelligent, but they must be the most dedicated. So when an executive understands how to develop people who possess the proper skills, make and communicate decisions, and correct mistakes, they will be unstoppable. I am sure that you are a star performer in your current line of work, but you will never be an effective manager until you develop the ability to allow that same work to be completed by someone under your direct control." (Mr. B. – Information Technology)

107. "Too often students believe because they receive an education they can lead people and run a business. Business schools instill that false sense of hope in students. Strategic management is a human art. It has nothing to do with books. It is something you cannot teach. Management is a personality. It is about getting people to work for you and to be happy at the same time. It makes people want to work for you, while not being too easy on employees. People respect managers who give praise and show respect, but also who are tough when times call for it. People either have it or they don't. It is an art, rather than a science." (Mr. B. – Retailing)

108. "Management is really about leading your employees. Decisions can be made, but they are meaningless if you cannot make your employees respond and become motivated to a new course of action." (Mr. H. – Construction)

144. "I'm going to give you the same advice that was given to me. There are five good qualities that you must develop before you get into an executive position. They are as follows: 1) Train your managers and employees effectively. This will limit you being on top of your employees each and every day. 2) You need to know how to lead. A company looks for a strong leader in a business setting to lead the company in an

upward direction. 3) You need to hire well. Hiring competent personnel to do a job can make or break a CEO. 4) You need to motivate well. Finding a way to motivate your employees will help the overall performance of the company. 5) You need to fire well. One day you might have to fire your best friend. You better make sure you can do that. I feel if you obtain these qualities that I have given you, you will climb the corporate ladder. If you don't, you are going to slide down the corporate ladder." (Mr. C. – Retailing)

153.   "Managers must know what their employees are working on. This relates especially to looking for symptoms of underlying problems. People don't usually want to talk about the issues giving them problems. Instead of being forthright about their failures or challenges, moral people won't cover them up, but they will avoid talking about them. Part of the leader's job is to know what his or her employees should be talking about. If an employee avoids that topic, the manager must ask the hard questions to get the employee to open up and reveal the whole picture. Shifts in the conversation dynamic are another symptom that something isn't right with an employee. I have experienced defensive employees who were normally very open. After some probing, the employee opens up about problems at work or outside of work. No matter where the root of the problem is, if it is affecting an employee's work time, it is a manager's responsibility to respond to the problem." (Mr. L. – Healthcare)

159.   "Do not take your responsibilities lightly. Be serious about your work, and people will take your work seriously. But have a sense of humor. People are

put at ease when they can deal with someone with a sense of humor, and it can help people to draw to you and look up to you." (Mr. J. – Conglomerate)

160.   "The first skill to develop is leadership. This is an imperative skill that business school does not necessarily teach you. It is a skill you have to develop personally and really work at. Also, remember that different types of people require different kinds of leaders. Someone who leads attorneys may need different attributes and tactics from someone who is leading marketing people." (Mr. M. – Entertainment & Media)

161.   "Unless you are alone, in a locked room without a phone, you are going to have to interact with people. The better you can become at relating to people and the more empathetic you can become with what is going on in their lives, the better manager you will become. Sure you will have to be able to manage tasks as well, but the bulk of the job will be spent working with peers, employees, customers, etc." (Mr. B. – Financial Services)

162.   "Learn to manage people! This is the end product of management. Management always boils down to people. An organization is a human construct, and is only as good as the people within. Nurture and expand the human talents within an organization." (Mr. T. – Hospitality)

164.   "The leadership of an organization must set a level playing field for all the employees. As long as it is clearly laid out what is expected of people, you can get around having winners and losers in the corporate

struggle for organizational leadership and organizational development. As long as people understand, and it is clearly laid out what is expected of them, then I think you can have a level playing field. All you can do is create a level playing field so that people don't feel like they are disenfranchised or being treated unfairly. Then each individual has to perform. I think the key is to make sure you are providing that level playing field, and you are communicating what their goals and objectives are, and then measuring them fairly against those. When companies fail, it is mostly due to a lack of leadership." (Mr. S. – Food & Agriculture)

178. "Decentralize power. You need to allow your team or managers to manage, so you should position yourself as a coach. Teach them how to manage so you can have more time to focus." (Mr. R. – Manufacturing)

181. "You must see to it that everyone in the organization is working towards your core strategy. This is accomplished by holding employees accountable at all levels of the organization." (Mr. F. – Healthcare)

184. "Be flexible. The human element of management is what MBAs truly need to understand. They must be flexible, good at communicating, and love a challenge. Do not forget how important incentives are to meeting your objectives. The human element is the hardest part to master. Nobody truly understands what it means to be a manager until they have to fire someone that they really like." (Mr. G. – Manufacturing)

193. "Big fancy strategies are not the way I run this business. I focus on the people, set a general direction, and stay out of the way. It's like being in the back of a canoe. When you are in a canoe, the last thing you want to do is paddle too much because you will overcorrect the canoe. Instead, you look at where you want to go and make occasional small strokes to redirect the canoe." (Mr. H. – Manufacturing)

194. "No matter how much time you spend thinking about, worrying about, focusing on, questioning the value of, and evaluating people, it won't be enough. People are the only thing that matters, and the primary thing you should think about, because when that part is right, everything else works. Knowing how to motivate your employees is part of the art that goes into strategic management. Each individual in the organization must be handled differently, in a manner where you are basically customizing your approach for each particular situation." (Mr. J. – Financial Services)

206. "What I often find lacking in managers is the ability to finish things. MBAs need to understand that if they are responsible for something, they need to 'know' that it has been done. Too often, people will delegate a task to someone else and assume it is either done or is no longer their responsibility. You can't do everything yourself and must rely on other people for help, but you must also retain responsibility and make sure that you know it has been completed rather than assuming so. This involves knowing all of the criteria that need to be completed for the task, and ensuring that they are communicated effectively." (Ms. K. – Business Services)

208. "An effective strategic manager makes employees feel at all levels that they are not just a cog in a wheel, unimportant, or simply mechanical. Rather, every employee needs to have an emotional attachment to the job that they are performing. I believe in developing a partnership with them, and whenever possible, giving them tangible evidence that they are needed and respected in the decision making process." (Mr. C. – Healthcare)

218. "Probably if you interviewed two or three other people there would be two or three other opinions for that question. That's what makes leadership and management so interesting; there are really no absolute answers. Sometimes we don't know what the answer is until we're done; sometimes we do really well at it, and sometimes we don't. It all comes down to patience. I think good work ethic, integrity, character, and doing the right things at all times is important. But my favorite thing of all time is this: When I walk into the bank I think, 'What would the bank be like if everyone in here acted like me?' It all comes back to my attitude. If I bring in a bad attitude into work, we're going to have a horrible day. Employees won't be happy, and our customers are not going to like us. But if I come in with a positive attitude, a positive will and good habits, that will flow onto other people and they will do an exciting job, and our customers will want to do business here. That is probably my all time favorite. 'What would this place be like if everyone here acted like me?'" (Mr. C. – Financial Services)

222. "One thing a lot of people don't think about is the humbleness. The reason is people need to feel

important, and they need to feel like they are the key person to that organization. A leader must be humble enough to be able to make each employee feel this way. A leader must have confidence; however, confidence can result in arrogance, and arrogance doesn't make a good leader." (Mr. M. – Retailing)

229. "Be respectful of others; it's the old adage of the golden rule and 'How you treat people on the way up will have an impact on the way down.'" (Mr. T. – Consumer Products)

231. "Delegation is a great talent to learn as an executive. Getting other people to do the things that need to be done will allow you to do what you need to get accomplished in a timely manner. You have to motivate your workers to contribute meaningful work to the corporation. And I am adamant about this: either care about people, or you better be pretty damn smart. If you do not care for your employees, they will not be there to help you when you need it. If you do not care about people and they know that, then that is a situation when being a CEO can be a real lonely life." (Mr. H. – Consumer Products)

252. "To become a true leader, be confident about what you are doing and the reasons why you are doing it. Don't be a push-over, meaning don't let people come and change your mind about something you know is right. Also, organize your thoughts so that you don't have to sit and wait for something to come to you; go out and get it. Be in control of your actions. Be polite but aggressive, and earn respect by saying things that are correct and not just politically correct.

We must respect others' opinions and sometimes agree to disagree." (Mr. F. – Financial Services)

277.   "Put yourself in a position of leadership. Lead something, even if small. Be responsible for the outcome of something. That will get you the experience you need. When you are a leader, you influence others, and you are making right decisions. If you make wrong decisions, learn from them. Put yourself in pressure; it will give you a lot of experience." (Mr. P. – Retailing)

280.   "In school you have been given tools that are valuable but insufficient. You can assume, and are correct in the fact that you have a strong new perspective and a tool box. The key now is how you get people to join together, work together, and allow you to lead them forward. Never confuse or assume that leadership and management are the same things. An organization needs both, but a good manager will not necessarily make a good leader. That is okay. In order to be a successful CEO though, you need to be a good leader. When you start your career it is what you know that starts to drive your success. In the end, what you know becomes irrelevant and your true success is all about your ability to inspire and lead people." (Mr. S. – Information Technology)

287.   "The hardest thing you'll probably do in your career is hiring people. One of the hardest things you can do is hiring someone after three one-hour sessions. If you get it right more than 30% of the time, then you're doing pretty well. We use all kinds of methods, but I have found that the interviews that are not done face-to-face are usually more predictive of good

outcomes because there is less bias about the way someone looks. Final decisions are still based on face-to-face, but written assignments and phone interviews are valuable tools in selecting personnel." (Mr. G. – Manufacturing)

287. "Find ways to demonstrate to your staff what to expect, and recognize them in real-time when they do well. Teach them how to manage by learning through lots of small lessons rather than only through big events." (Mr. G. – Manufacturing)

290. "Leadership is envisioning, setting direction, aligning, motivating and inspiring actions of a group of people together – sometimes even moving beyond their collective or individual imagination. Management is planning, staffing, budgeting, problem solving and controlling to get the best out of every individual based on their make-up. Be aware of both, and be aware of when you are in one or the other mode. And tell people which mode you are in. They will understand you. Neither leadership nor management is a manifestation of a mysterious magical touch, voodoo or personal charisma, intelligence or style. Rather, both are pragmatic processes; you understand them and move yourself and colleagues through them. You must lead with explicit purpose, and manage with explicit consistency. Also, you may want to read 'Leading with Purpose' by Richard Ellsworth, which talks about much of the philosophies we have discussed." (Dr. M. – Healthcare)

297. "Don't ever underestimate people skills because you are always going to need those. Be interested in what the people you work with are doing.

Don't just be interested in yourself." (Mr. R. – Hospitality)

301. "If I could give you one thing to take away from here today, it is when you are a manager make sure you have good people. Be open, honest with them, but be firm. If you are open and you are honest, they cannot criticize you for being firm because you are being fair. And then care about them and let them know you care about them by your actions." (Mr. G. – Energy, Mining & Materials)

303. "Develop the skill of hiring and selecting the best possible people for each spot. You know, you have to learn how to give up authority and let other people develop and do what they are best at doing. You help remove the roadblocks for them to be successful. I think that is what is really key for building a good unit, a good organization, a good department or company or whatever it is. Develop that skill of determining whether people are going to add to, be mediocre, or subtract from the organization when you are interviewing them or considering their hire. Then develop the knack to work with them in a way that will help them be successful; then let them run with what they know how to do best. I'm not sure that is taught in MBA school. I didn't learn it in school." (Mr. K. – Conglomerate)

306. "People are the real assets in the organization, but managing people with so many constraints in a company is the most challenging task. If you can manage people, you can manage the company to a certain extent. Different people have different priorities, so it requires complex managerial skills to

bring everybody onto the same page." (Mr. S. – Entertainment & Media)

316. "Well, I think that the more you understand people, the better off you are. And let me tell you, it's a never ending educational process (laughs). But just realize that you don't get ahead in life by stepping over and stepping on other people. The best thing in the world that I think you can do as you climb the ladder of success is having your hand down pulling other people up with you. The more people around you that you can help be successful, the more you are going to be successful. Just realize that I don't care exactly what kind of work you're doing; dealing with people and how you deal with people will determine your success. It's something you're going to be faced with, just learning good people skills. I tell you, if I were you I'd get the book 'How to Win Friends and Influence People.' I've given that to my son. I read it years and years ago. I've got it sitting right over there. I'm reading it again. It was written back in the 1930's, but it is the best human relations book you'll ever read. And if you can consistently do what is in that book, you'll do fine. I promise you." (Mr. B. – Healthcare)

321. "You've got to have good interpersonal skills, and think about how people are responding to what you're doing. The main focus has to be how a given person is looking at what you're doing, and how they respond accordingly. You can't come into the workplace saying, 'You're not following the Vroom-Jago model of leadership.' People right out of college have to gain their peers' respect right off the bat. You have to get in there and roll up your sleeves and work along with the people you hope to lead. If you can do

this, once you move up you don't have to gain their respect strictly as a leader because you already gained their respect as a co-worker. You live and die by your people, so they have to know that you appreciate what they do for you. So don't be embarrassed to thank people for the small things. In the end you will be a much better leader in every situation." (Mr. C. – Utilities)

324. "Be open, flexible, always trying to improve your people skills, trying to improve yourself, and making yourself someone who people are always going to want to be around. Develop yourself into a leader that way." (Mr. S. – Financial Services)

348. "As a manager, your employees aren't there to help you; you are there to help them." (Mr. K. – Business Services)

353. "Management is not for everyone. It is very difficult to be able to manage people as well as be expected to run a successful business. People are unpredictable, so you must be able to adapt to every situation and reach suitable and justifiable decisions. The most important thing is to surround yourself with people who are brighter than you are." (Mr. K. – Consumer Services)

365. "I think you should always look to challenge your management and be willing to get involved. I'm a strong believer in employee involvement. We need to listen. Don't be afraid to challenge your management and get involved. One thing I've never been afraid to do is step up to the plate and just

challenge individuals. I've never been afraid of a good challenge." (Mr. M. – Utilities)

368.   "Learn the skills – and you may have to have a natural knack for it – but learn the skills of people development. Learn how to get the most out of people. Learn how to allow them to feel free to communicate ideas and thoughts. You create a synergy where ideas are flowing. I can sit around and think of stuff all damn day, but I can sit in a meeting and hear ideas and wonder, 'Why didn't I think of that?' You have to use your people – I don't mean that in a bad way." (Mr. D. – Retailing)

370.   "Surround yourself with good people and give them the encouragement and the tools they need to do the job and then let them do it. If you have someone who is not performing, deal with that quickly. You will be able to tell in just a few weeks if the person just doesn't have it in them. If that is the case, the best thing you can do is to terminate them right away. Second chances seldom work, and in the meantime you are bringing down your entire team." (Ms. I. – Food & Agriculture)

383.   "Develop real sensitivity around how people are different. Where I see people fail in organizations is where they can't quite get around the fact that we aren't all the same. Some people you know are real drivers and they can appear to be insensitive. Other people have their heads in the clouds all the time and you wonder if they get anything done. Understanding people – how they are different, how to communicate with them, how things can get sort of sideways, and all that kind of stuff – that is really important, because

at the end of the day you want to manage work activity and that usually means you are managing people. People are the hardest part. I'd love this business if I didn't have to have people and I didn't have employees, just customers. In our case, I have managers I have to coach. They just don't know how to be confrontational. Someone can be screwing off right in their midst and they will not say something to that person. On the other hand, I've had managers that hit roadblocks and can't think creatively about how to get around them. So I have to coach them. I have managers who have a hard time delegating. They want to do it all, or they will pick favorites. I know you can delegate to two people, but not these two people. All this stuff is absolute crux to being a great leader." (Mr. V. – Retailing)

386. "It is imperative to understand that an excellent strategic manager knows the people side of the company, understands the importance of teams, has a ruthless nature in recruiting talent, and focuses on succession planning. It is especially important that a strategic manager thinks about the future and is actively identifying and developing the next candidate to take their job." (Mr. S. – Utilities)

389. "If you are a middle manager in a large organization or a smaller organization, I think one of the key things – one of the key jobs of the manager – is to be able to explain to the people on my team how what we're doing ties into the strategy of the company: 'Why are we doing this?' Because I think people are more motivated and more committed when they understand how what they are doing fits, rather than when they think they are just working. It's like the old

story about the guy laying bricks and someone comes up to him and asks, 'What are you doing?' There are two answers to this. He can say, 'I'm laying bricks,' or he can say, 'I'm building a church.' One is a much different view of the work than the other. So if you walked up to one of our software engineers here and said, 'What are you doing?' He could say, 'Well I'm trying to develop a routine that would do this...' But we hope that he would say, 'I'm doing this because it fits into the overall scheme of this product which is a part of our strategy of helping to keep people safe.' I think one of the key things to understanding strategic management is to be able to understand the strategy of the company so that you can explain to your team how what you are doing tactically ties into that strategy." (Mr. C. – Information Technology)

391.   "Everyone in the organization is responsible for strategy development, not just the CEO. It's about people, strategy, and getting things done. So many parts of it come down to culture and people. The leaders of an organization, the CEO, and even the President of the United States, set a lot of the culture of what people under them are going to do. In the case of Enron, there were people at the top who didn't have integrity, and that wound its way down through the ranks." (Dr. K. – Healthcare)

405.   "It's pretty straightforward. You should understand that people and companies both have feelings. Every company and every person is different and needs to be treated differently. Learn to treat everyone with respect. There's a saying, 'People will forget what you say; people will forget what you do, but they never forget how you made them feel.' If you

treat others with respect, you'll find people will remember that, and respect you in return. And that definitely will make a difference in the future." (Mr. B. – Food & Agriculture)

423. "People will disappoint you. It is part of the learning experience, maybe the greatest part of the learning experience. I have had some very difficult situations; it is just part of life. When people disappoint you, you can't feel, 'Well how can anyone ever do that?' That is why you never want to put any employee on a pedestal. It's not a perfect world. We don't deal in a perfect world, and people are going to disappoint you. I think sometimes people don't prepare themselves for that." (Mr. H – Consumer Services)

429. "It is vital to hire good people because the quality of the people you hire creates positive outcomes for the company. Therefore, you have to allow your employees to do the job you hired them for; do not be a micromanager. The CEO always needs to be open to the advice and knowledge of their employees because there is a good chance that he is not the smartest person in the organization. You must expect a lot from your people and hold them accountable. Then you should value their achievements and enhance your relationships with them. The more effort you put into valuing your employees, the more respect they will have for you, and they will be proud to work for your company." (Mr. R. – Construction)

430. "What sets a company apart from one that's mediocre is the people. Developing the ability to

interact with people – to influence people – is critically important. It's being able to do it in a way that's not heavy handed, being able to articulate an idea. It's the softer, people-side of an organization. Those who are higher performers have mastered that side of the business. Interactive people skills are crucial." (Mr. R. – Consumer Products)

443. "Management is really about people, people, people. If you've got five employees and one is bad, that's 20% of your workforce. Get rid of them! But don't get rid of them by getting into a fight with them. Get rid of them on your time, not their time. By that I mean bring someone else in, train them, then let your other employee go. You will have an employee, and someone will come and say, 'They're late every day; they take a long lunch; they don't produce; they call in sick or lot; they this and that.' And you'd say, 'I'd let that guy go.' What 13 year-old wouldn't? That's when most management lets people go, when a child would have done it! A mediocre leader, though, they wouldn't do it. But how many companies succeed with mediocre people? How many basketball teams win championships with mediocre players? The biggest thing I would be talking to people about today is to take someone's hand and let them move on. You don't have to be ugly. You don't have to let them down. You don't have to make them feel bad; but you can let them go. They could be a good neighbor, but they just won't work in my company." (Mr. R. – Transportation)

445. "Everyone needs to understand that it takes time and a great deal of experience before you can effectively be a leader of a company. I was able to watch my father and follow his lead for many years as

a young business man. When I first started working at the bank, my father taught me that the way to lead was to be demanding and have full control over my employees. He came from the 'school of hard knocks' and believed no one should have anything just handed to them. While this is still true today – people should have to work hard for what they want in life – I have realized there is a different way to achieve these results. People today are smarter and we live in a diverse world. People won't work for someone who is harsh and controlling. They don't want to be disrespected or put down. Today it seems that people work better by being built up and given compliments. Employees want reassurance and a sense of achievement. People like to feel that they are a part of a team, and they know they can come to me for advice. Loyalty and caring for employees is imperative. By letting them know that you are concerned with their lives makes all the difference in the world. So always be kind to everyone you meet. People remember you by how you initially treat them. Be kind to your employees and your customers. Caring about the people around you means knowing something about their personal lives. Really get to know the people you meet and work with each day. They are the ones that help run what you lead, so be a respectful and loyal leader." (Mr. R. – Financial Services)

447. "It's real easy to say that I am going to improve the attitude of the associates here, but how am I going to measure it? And how am I going to know if we achieved it? Beware of simply saying at the end of the year, 'Well I think they are happier.'" (Mr. S. – Healthcare)

449.   "Always be fair with everyone that you deal with. That doesn't mean that you don't hold people accountable, but it does mean that you treat them with the respect and decency that you would want someone to extend to you. Always keep that in mind and good things will happen to you." (Mr. M. – Consumer Services)

453.   "Don't be intimidated by people that are smarter than you are. Employ them; learn from them, and utilize their abilities to add to your company's success." (Mr. A. – Manufacturing)

456.   "Honestly, you first have to understand fully on the ground what and who you are managing. You have to get to know the people. Too many people treat others like boxes. First you have to get out to the people that are running your product and understand them, see what drives them. Some people are driven by money; some are driven by other things, but everyone is driven by something. Find what drives somebody, and absolutely don't put everybody in the same box. You have to become a coach." (Mr. K. – Hospitality)

459.   "At its core, management today is the same as it was 200 years ago. It's getting people to do what you want them to do. It's all about getting things done through other people. How you motivate people hasn't changed in a long time. People are motivated through a combination of compensation, recognition, consideration, and ownership in something beyond just being an employee. Their effort needs to be appreciated and valued, and they need to feel that. There's no one way to motivate people, but employee

motivation is essential. It does you no good to have the best strategic plan in the world if you don't have motivated people who are willing to make the effort to implement it." (Mr. B. – Financial Services)

473. "It's important to understand what it is your employees need, both personally and professionally because they need to be reaching their professional goals. So you have to set and define the overarching strategic goal and direction, and then make sure your employees have the tools to grow professionally so that they can achieve those goals." (Mr. F. – Manufacturing)

479. "When I got that huge diploma on the wall over there, I carried it into my first CEO job and tried to find the perfect place to put it in my office. The retiring CEO said to me, 'They don't care what you know; they just want you to care about them.' Demonstrate first that you care about people you are leading. Every CEO I know who has been fired from their position knew the science of strategic management, knew financial analysis, but were fired due to interpersonal skills problems or busted relationships. There is not enough science in leadership that will help you succeed unless they know you care." (Mr. T. – Healthcare)

485. "Hire the best people. If you do that well, everything else will fall into place. Good people are cheap in the long-run because they can take on more and do it right the first time. I wish I could have gone after the best in the beginning, but money was tight and I thought I was making the right decisions to hire based on our salary budget alone. Also, I was too slow

to fire in the beginning, but I got smart. I'm now more discerning about hiring and faster to fire when I know someone's not going to work out. As CEO, it's key to put the best, smartest people in all areas." (Ms. G. – Manufacturing)

505.	"Human relation principles are critical in every industry. Always be about recognizing employees and their accomplishments, and encouraging them to grow, and getting them to rally in tough times by keeping them positive. Band together as a team to get the job done." (Ms. L. – Consumer Products)

522.	"Make no excuses. If look at my income statement, my number one cost is excuses. That's what I tell people. Don't allow yourself to fall into that trap. Yet you do need to live with compassion, but not to the point where you are hurting a person. You can't just give them everything; you have to let them get the best out of life by making their own way, earning, accomplishing. You can't dumb people down, but you just have to try and understand people and their circumstances. So your understanding has to come by putting yourself in their shoes and trying to help in that circumstance, and doing everything you can in the place that they are at." (Mr. M. – Food & Agriculture)

523.	"Never underestimate the ability of people to rise up and contribute to the success of an organization. I say that because it is not always that the person with the three degrees hanging on their wall in their nice frames. It could be the power of the front line worker who can contribute and the value of that worker." (Mr. K. – Food & Agriculture)

525.   "One thing that took me nearly 50 years to fully understand is that people are the most important part of any business." (Mr. W. – Transportation)

534.   "You've got to do more than the next guy. You've got to be there and do it with a positive attitude because a positive attitude can take you a long way if you're a hard worker and you're honest. It amazes me that our schools don't have one course on attitude. I could be the smartest guy in the world and have all sorts of knowledge about business, but if I just treated you like hell when you came up here, I wouldn't do very good at anything, and you wouldn't want to be around me." (Mr. T. – Food & Agriculture)

560.   "Listen more than you talk. The customer makes the company, but the employees get the customers." (Mr. C. – Entertainment & Media)

561.   "Put yourself in some position of leadership. Lead something, even if small. Be responsible for the outcome of something. That will get you valuable experience. When you are a leader, you influence others, and you are making decisions. If you make wrong decisions, learn from them. Put yourself into pressure; it will give you a lot of experience." (Mr. P. – Consumer Products)

564.   "You have been given tools that are valuable but insufficient. You can assume that you have a strong new perspective and a tool box. The key now is how you get people to join together, work together, and allow you to lead them forward. Never confuse or assume that leadership and management are the same thing. An organization needs both, but a good

manager will not necessarily make a good leader. That is okay. In order to be a successful CEO though, you need to be a good leader. When you start your career it is what you know that starts to drive your success. But in the end, what you know becomes irrelevant and your true success is all about your ability to inspire and lead people." (Mr. S. – Manufacturing)

LEARNING

What intrigues you? What fascinates you? What are you curious about? A lot?! You've got potential! Nourish that. Focus it on becoming more and more useful for others. You're on your way!

17.   "Listen to people more than you talk. There is a wealth of knowledge to be learned from everyone. That's how I have learned all that I have, by listening." (Mr. D. – Business Services)

18.   "Stay humble. At your stage of my life, I was much like a sponge and was still in the 'Growth Stage' of my career and life. There are many things to learn in the business world that cannot be taught in books or lectures. So stay humble and listen to others. Go into a field that you are very interested in. Learn as much as you can about the field; this will give you intimate knowledge of the field and enable you to move forward." (Mr. A. – Financial Services)

29.   "Learn how to think and learn on your own. Think independently; it teaches you how to think deeply." (Mr. D. – Energy, Mining & Materials)

35.   "Knowledge is infinite. Never think you have learned enough. Humility helps you absorb more knowledge, while arrogance keeps you away from improvement." (Mr. B. – Financial Services)

36.   "You will never stop learning, never stop trying new ideas and exploring new methods for solving problems." (Mr. B. – Construction)

Learning

87.   "Never quit learning. Work is a learning platform. The Catch-22 is that you won't understand until you learn, but once you've learned you wish you would have known it to begin with." (Mr. K. – Manufacturing)

92.   "One of the most important things to learn is that while there are necessary tools for a person to possess to be a successful strategic manager, these tools are not sufficient to guarantee success. A person must have experience and acquire tools over time to be a more effective strategic thinker. The learning process is never complete. Learning allows for constant and continuous improvement to the organization. So a successful strategic manager must stay current and know what is going on in the organization and the environment to adequately deal with changes." (Mr. M. – Manufacturing)

129.   "Everything you do in life is an opportunity and a building experience, whether in the course of work, personal affairs, social settings, or even school. Things happen on a daily basis that you can apply to your objectives. You should not go through life blind, but instead capitalize off of these experiences and discover how they correlate to you. Be willing to tackle hard assignments. When entering into your career, if members of a task force are being recruited, show willingness to take part. Over time, through a combination of all these experiences, you will become a source of information yourself, and you can truly say that you've educated yourself." (Mr. W. – Financial Services)

131. "Never stop learning. Whether in or out of the business world, pick something that intrigues you and expand your strategic knowledge of it. When you know about things that others don't, you hold the power to create need." (Mr. E. – Entertainment & Media)

139. "College students know a little bit about devotion in my opinion, because they have committed to and completed a four-year course of study. But that absolutely pales in comparison to the course of study you are about to undertake for the rest of your life. Every day for the rest of your life will be a learning experience, and the world will be your classroom." (Mr. C. – Energy, Mining & Materials)

161. "You can't be afraid to ask questions. Asking questions doesn't make you look stupid, it keeps you from looking stupid." (Mr. B. – Financial Services)

165. "Stick to your guns. You must be intrinsically comfortable with the path you need to take. You can never learn everything you need to know from other people. You can blend others' thoughts or ideas into what you want to be, but ultimately it comes from within." (Mr. J. – Retailing)

208. "Management is all about constantly learning no matter how experienced you are in your position. It would be erroneous to think you know everything about the business. Technology is changing at such a rapid pace, so one must be aware of things happening around them as well as in other industries. Other industries are important because the triumphs or failures they are having could potentially spill into your

Learning

industry, so you must be aware of that. I also would emphasize reading religiously to stay in touch. Read journals, newspapers, publications, and anything that has the potential to help or hinder your company or industry. You must constantly keep abreast of what's occurring in the business world, and how it is applicable to you. One cannot be an effective manager without being well-informed, inquisitive, and know what's happening." (Mr. C. – Healthcare)

229. "You are always learning, but be thirsty to learn more. There's an old saying about the smartest man understanding what he doesn't know. Treat every day as a learning experience." (Mr. T. – Consumer Products)

233. "Understand that a lot of what you do early on is a means to an end. I didn't particularly like my job at the start, but my idea of it was that it was a way of getting a good understanding of the way businesses work and what matters to management. So I thought, 'If I get reasonably good at this, I'll have some knowledge a lot of people don't have.' I was willing to put the time and effort into my job so that in the longer term I could use it for other things. There are plenty of people that don't like the prospect of that. But everything you do early on can have value later as you understand that you are learning things other people don't know. This can have great value if you learn to accept it." (Mr. D. – Business Services)

242. "There is no such thing as a job that you can't learn from. It may be a temporary job. It may be that you are working a coffee shop to make some extra money, or you are changing tires at a tire shop. Every job teaches you something; you learn about people

149

and pick up different skills. So, if you treat every job as if it is going to lead somewhere, even if in your mind it is a dead end job, you are going to be better off. You can learn how to deal with troublesome coworkers, bosses, and customers. Everything builds and builds. If you don't think that a job is a waste of time, then you can learn something from it. You will meet people; you will learn things. It's hard to understand that each job will give you a different skill until you have been working for a while, but then you will begin to see the benefit of all the different work experiences. In my case, I've had a few jobs that would be considered lousy, but I learned a ton from those lousy jobs. I've learned how not to be – how not be a boss, how not to treat the consumer. But I have also learned the right ways to do things. I learned the right ways to talk to people properly, and how to just be a good employee. If you can't go into a job at Starbucks and learn something about customer service, then you aren't engaging in the experience. However, if you are willing to go into a job to learn, then that job, even though it will not be your career defining job, will lead you to become better at what you do next. Sometimes it may not be the job that needs to change, it may just be your attitude. This is because you've talked yourself into not liking it. You have to have the attitude of 'I am going to be the best I can be at my job.' Otherwise it is a waste of time. You have to take a positive outlook on each job. You can have fun and learn even at jobs that are not necessarily ideal or career-based." (Mr. O. – Manufacturing)

249. "Strive to keep learning. There are always an unlimited amount of opportunities to learn and grow." (Mr. F. – Healthcare)

256. "As an amateur entering into the world, you should never stop reading." (Mr. G. – Construction)

259. "Learn from the people who you can observe, whether they are doing things right or whether they are doing things wrong. Learn from what they are doing right or from what they are doing wrong. I've always tried to do that from the very early days of my career, and I have learned from good managers and from bad managers. I think that is very critical." (Mr. J. – Financial Services)

262. "Never confuse rewards and learning." (Mr. C. – Healthcare)

263. "It is always good to embrace learning in any situation. The more you know, the more valuable you become." (Ms. H. – Financial Services)

272. "I've been able to shape a great part of what I've done in large part due to reading. You can learn so much from other people's successes and failures. The easiest thing you can do is to learn from what other people before you have done. I'll do it to my dying day!" (Dr. H. – Business Services)

283. "One of the best ways to learn is to teach. I found for me, one of the helpful things for my development was doing United Way Campaigns and finding myself in leadership volunteering in not-for-profit organizations. They are always looking for talented people who want to do it. Personally, it really helped my development because I was exposed to some stuff far sooner than I would have been otherwise. As you are bringing value to a not-for-profit,

with the right one, you will be getting a lot out of it. What I found with my community and volunteer work, the more I put into it, the more I got out of it." (Mr. S. – Entertainment & Media)

285. "My advice? Learn as much as much as you can. Pick a firm with a purpose, values and people you admire. Learn as much as you can from them. You can never stop learning. You may laugh at your parents because of their lack of technological experience, but you will not be young forever. Your ability to learn, and to continue to learn, will be an important asset." (Mr. M. – Consumer Products)

288. "Use what you are being taught as a great resource. You have an opportunity to gain so much knowledge – take it. Don't stop learning. You never stop learning. I have a true desire to learn so I am never afraid in a room – whether with my peers, or whether it be with people I am supposed to be leading – I have never had a problem saying, 'I don't get this. I don't understand this. Somebody help me understand this.' Or, 'Somebody help me understand; I need to learn what we are talking about here so I can be involved in the decision making process. Right now, I don't have the knowledge to do it. So, this is another opportunity for me to learn.' Don't stop learning. It's cliché, but don't think you ever know it all." (Mr. H. – Hospitality)

290. "Your education has created a framework in which you can grow professionally. Use your education as a framework, like a plant uses a lattice to grow. Don't look at it as a hurdle that you've passed or something that you had to suffer through just to get

more letters attached to the end of your name. Continue to expand your knowledge base; always read anything you can get your hands on about strategic management. Never stop growing and never stop learning." (Dr. M. – Healthcare)

296. "First of all, you have to realize that when you come out, you've got more to learn than you have learned in your last 20 years of education. All that you have done is prepare yourself to take a step in the door. If you go in with that attitude, there is a likelihood of success." (Mr. H. – Financial Services)

300. "Remember that you have got to keep learning. What you have learned is in many cases a framework to help you evaluate situations and help you make decisions. You're going to learn the rest of your life. You need to keep learning, whether it's learning to speak Spanish if you don't now, because that's going to be incredibly useful to you. Or whether you spend some time learning more about History, which is going to be an incredible asset for you as time goes along. Understand more about Economics than most people. If you're running an organization, show people in the organization that you're concerned about continuing to learn because that makes it easier to convince them that they need to continue to learn." (Mr. B. – Consumer Products)

318. "In order to stay on top of your work and continue to lead and grow your company, you always have to stay plugged in to what is going on. This is not to say that you cannot have your down time, but you still need to understand that your company is still functioning when you are not there. By staying

plugged in, you keep a finger on the pulse to make sure that everything is running smoothly. Being a good CEO is not a nine-to-five job; it is a job that requires diligent effort and a strong backbone. Staying plugged in to what is going on and how the company is performing is what you need to know. Truly, there really are no more nine-to-five jobs. In order to grow and succeed, you are going to have to put in more effort, and stay more 'plugged in' than ever before. Competition in all industries has become so complex that the forty-hour workweek has passed us by. To get ahead in such complex markets, staying plugged in is crucial to your success. This is not to say that work needs to be your life and nothing else, but it is necessary to always have an eye on what is going on." (Mr. R. – Energy, Mining & Materials)

320. "With everything you do you need to ask yourself, 'What am I learning? How do I develop?' because your main goal is to develop as an individual." (Mr. G. – Manufacturing)

321. "You have to be open to learning about leadership and motivating people in every aspect of your life, not just within the workplace. It's always good to get involved in professional and civic organizations and take leadership roles within them because that's where you will develop a lot of your most valuable leadership skills. When you're involved with a civic organization which is made up of volunteers, the only way that you can get them to work with you and for you is to gain their respect and show them a common vision to get them to work together. With employees, you're paying them, so it's much easier to motivate them. But with volunteer

organizations, you have to figure out different ways, usually through trial-and-error, to get them to do the things they may not necessarily want to do. Through participation in those organizations, you get to observe other effective leaders in action, and you can learn very quickly the ways they lead and which ways are effective and the ones that are not." (Mr. C. – Utilities)

327. "Pay attention. In other words, listen to people, learn, absorb, work really hard, and make sure you understand what's going on. Absorb everything around you so you can understand why things are happening, and that's where you build your experience." (Mr. H. – Hospitality)

332. "Leadership is a learned skill set that takes time and experience. Read, study, and try many different approaches for different people and situations. Sometimes we learn the most from painful situations. Read good books and attend classes yearly to grow and learn." (Ms. R. – Information Technology)

334. "My piece of advice is to continuously work to improve. Whether participating in optional training, reading books, taking classes, or whatever improvement opportunities that the individual is able to identify, work to constantly improve." (Mr. S. – Information Technology)

336. "I would tell you to read, read, read. I tell that to a lot of people. I recommend every morning that you grab a newspaper. Every Sunday, without fail, grab a *New York Times* or a *Wall Street Journal* and read it

cover to cover. You can find many interesting articles and can learn so much." (Mr. K. – Manufacturing)

339.   "The more you know, the more valuable you are, and it will be recognized. People have this misconception that management doesn't know who's doing what. That's wrong; management knows, even at my level. They think I don't know, but I do. (Ms. H. – Financial Services)

341.   "I would be a student. You can't quit learning once you graduate; you have to be a student of the industry you are in. You have to learn everything you can learn about it, and then continue to learn from the people you are working for and with – and certainly from outside resources, books, seminars, the internet, and wherever you can get more information to help you gain insight into your industry. You need to keep learning to become competent in your industry. Anybody beginning a career needs to work on building their competence because in the end they will never become the CEO unless they really know the industry they are in." (Mr. D. – Retailing)

343.   "You will ultimately rise to the level of your inability. If you allow yourself to constantly learn new things and new methods for doing things, would you not continually rise? At this point you have the basic information for the field you intend to enter; however, you still have a lot of learning ahead of you. Allow yourself to build a firm foundation beyond what you think you already know." (Mr. M. – Healthcare)

358.   "Leaders are readers. Always be reading; always be learning. Recognize the distinction between

management and leadership. Early in your career you have to focus on technical training, but look for opportunities to migrate toward leadership. You've got to learn your discipline first, then you can move to leadership. You've got to be focused on helping others; your passion shouldn't be just to learn more for the sake of learning more. Rather, let your passion be to learn more so that you can help more." (Mr. M. – Entertainment & Media)

371. "What I'd tell you today is, first of all, read all these great books. Gobble those things up. What I used to do when I was your age, I'd read Dale Carnegie's *How to Win Friends and Influence People*. And I'd have a highlighter, and I'd highlight anything that hit me right between the eyes. Like it said to never call a customer and say, 'I was in the neighborhood and I thought I'd drop by.' That makes the customer not feel important. So read all these books, and make your own lists and begin to get your own creed going. Dale Carnegie said this; Jack Welch lives by that, and I certainly live by that." (Mr. K. – Consumer Products)

382. "A good strategic manager stays well-read and up-to-date on what's going on in different industries. This keeps you ready for opportunities when they do arise." (Mr. F. – Conglomerate)

383. "Read a lot of books. I hate to say it, but when you ask me if I've had any success, it's because I've read a lot of books, number one. But at the same time, I probably only finish only one out of eight business books I start. I get four new business books a week, but I would argue most business books are way too long. Too many of them are written as self-help books even

though they may appear to be the mind of the market, or a third of them are entry level. But I think there is so much good information out there. Smaller books are so easy to hand out to your staff. I'm always amazed at the people in our distribution center that actually read these small books." (Mr. V. – Retailing)

392. "The most important piece of advice that can be given is to do everything you can to learn all that you can. Take in as many experiences as possible and try and learn something from all of them. The fact that time is on your side means that it is okay to fail, as long as you learn something from the experience and keep moving. The magic bullet, or formula for success is different for everyone. What works for the guy next to you might be the worst thing for you to do." (Mr. H. – Energy, Mining & Materials)

394. "Understand what you understand, then seek out the people and knowledge that will help you understand whatever else you believe is important to understand." (Mr. T. – Consumer Services)

395. "Education does not have to end when you get a diploma. You can continue learning by researching and talking to people in the business world. Something that every college student should learn is to not be afraid to ask questions. Do not hold back on anything." (Mr. S. – Manufacturing)

420. "Strive for continuous learning. I have the sense that a lot of students coming out of college think their studies are over; it's time to relax and put away the books. You should understand that although your formal education may have concluded, learning,

studying, reading, researching, investigating, it all continues, just in a different environment." (Mr. M. – Consumer Services)

428. "In a competitive environment, work ethic can overcome brilliance. A work ethic that is focused on continually learning and outworking the competition, those are two things that have made many people successful. Everyone has God-given skills that only take you so far; it comes down to how much you really want to succeed. Not many things are easy and painless." (Mr. C. – Business Services)

433. "Stay very curious. There's a saying that my father said to me growing up on a farm in Oklahoma. He said, 'You're only as smart as the ground you grew up on, but that doesn't mean you can't learn someone else's ground.' You will become successful by staying curious, understanding what you do know, and never ever being ashamed by asking a lot of questions." (Ms. T. – Consumer Products)

441. "Someone starting out should always do the best they can in order to obtain every little piece of valuable information they can." (Mr. B. – Energy, Mining & Materials)

446. "You certainly can't pick up your management style out of a book. You must keep your mind open and listen to others – customers, employees, etc. One must have lots of curiosity and constantly thinking, 'What's going on over there?'" (Mr. B. – Manufacturing)

450. "Continuously learn. Never stop learning. Continuous learning is very important because it keeps you vibrant. It makes you well-established. It makes you 'sustainable' within your business. And as well, when you leave your job you still have something that is yours. You can take that learning wherever you go; you can teach at a conference if you want, or you can be a mentor for someone else. Never stop learning. Don't miss that opportunity." (Ms. B. – Food & Agriculture)

460. "Education, education, education. I am such an advocate of going to school and getting as much information as possible for whatever you are doing. I have always been under the opinion that more school is always better. You may not learn everything you need to know in an educational setting, but it shows that you have the drive to continue, and that will open doors for you." (Mr. T. – Construction)

462. "Don't let any experiences go by without thinking about them and reliving them and thinking how you could have improved on those experiences. That's active learning. Do you have an on-board mechanism for self-development? Because the chances of you getting developed by somebody else are somewhat remote. Even if you find a good mentor, you still need to have those on-board mechanisms. So learning from experience – this whole concept of active learning – is absolutely vital." (Mr. B. – Consumer Products)

489. "Continue to nurture and kindle what I like to call intellectual curiosity – sensing, understanding, observing, watching, questioning the world around

you. It is the world you will be working in for the next forty years. The world will be much more globally influenced than anything I have seen, and how do you stay prepared for that? It is that constant search of broadening your skill set and understanding. Constantly ask, 'What have I learned? How can I do something better? How can we use what we learned and apply it to tomorrow?' Some may think they have found the answer. But no, there is not just one answer." (Mr. R. – Financial Services)

491.   "Once you get into the field that you really love, then you need to put all of your education and the strategic practices you have been taught into good use. Look at your resources, how does your education match the field that you are in? Treat your work like a sport; keep practicing and improving and never settle for just good enough. Success can only be achieved by those who seek it with the correct mindset." (Mr. S. – Construction)

495.   "An important thing to do is stay informed on current events. I have noticed that young people do not keep up with what is going on in the world, and that just blows my mind. You cannot be successful in business or in life if you do not stay informed. Plus, I have found that conversations with networking contacts or job interviews run more smoothly when you can intelligently discuss what is going on in the world, especially in your field of interest." (Mr. S. – Information Technology)

508.   "Read more than your work requires. Never stop learning. Nowadays, one career is no longer the norm; that is why you must continue to expand your

knowledge. Learn other positions and their responsibilities, but be sure to know and understand yours." (Mr. H. – Food & Agriculture)

513.   "Become the best at one specific thing. Become very good at two or more things." (Mr. D. – Business Services)

518.   "I've always been an avid reader. But I don't read novels. Continuous learning is important to every aspect of your life." (Ms. K. – Consumer Services)

520.   "Never stop learning or questing to learn. Every day I learn something new out of want and out of necessity. To stop learning means to stop growing, and this will cripple your career." (Mr. B. – Manufacturing)

522.   "Every time I talk to anyone I put myself in their shoes and I really listen. I really want to know their point of view regardless if they are right or wrong. I want to understand where they are at, what they are saying, and where they are coming from. From that I could glean something into my heart that could lighten me up and show me something different." (Mr. M. – Food & Agriculture)

523.   "Never stop learning from those around you. It's not just learning from those above you, but learning from customers, learning from the person pushing the broom or pushing the mop, learning from your competitors, learning from best practices both within your own industry, but also how another industry may relate to you and how those other companies have solved business strategies. Bring it all

back to your own organization and adapt the principles of that, the values of that. Truly at the end of the day never stop learning and keeping a focus on others and their best practices, and bring that back to your organization." (Mr. K. – Food & Agriculture)

524. "Continue to read. I cannot stress to you the benefits from continually reading. Right now I have about five different books on my nightstand. I have not finished all of them because I want to learn about something new every day. They are all exceptionally interesting thus far, but like I said, I have not finished them yet." (Mr. M. – Manufacturing)

540. "Get as much preparation as you can, and make yourself better by learning continuously. There are not any free lunches out there; you have to give it your best. If you don't want to put forth the effort, get out." (Mr. B. – Construction)

543. "Make sure that you get engaged with a company that has a very good training program that allows you to expand your education and knowledge and how it relates. Make sure that they allow you to continue to study while you are an employee." (Mr. M. – Healthcare)

547. "The world is much more global than it has ever been. Young professionals trying to penetrate the workforce must be knowledgeable on current foreign policies in order to truly understand the world and whatever industry they may be in. China and India specifically have a big impact." (Mr. L. – Energy, Mining & Materials)

548. "I find I spend a lot of time de-programming some of our agents. A lot of it is how they interact with other people in their department. I think it's just listening – listening to people who have been doing it for a long time. I find that the ones who ask the most questions are the ones who get ahead. You know, 'Do you have five minutes; can I ask you about this?' It's all about getting a knowledge of what's going on. I find our youngest associates don't ask enough questions. The ones that succeed do. The ones who ask for my help, they're the ones – they know they can't do it on their own. And that's great, I applaud that." (Mr. G. – Business Services)

557. "The most important thing when starting a career is to ask questions. Ask why things are done, what can be done to improve things, general business questions, whatever is necessary to gather all knowledge you can." (Mr. S. – Consumer Products)

558. "You will learn something new every day, so stay attentive." (Mr. H. – Transportation)

657. "Don't get caught up in fads and buzzwords. You should know the current fads in the marketplace but not let them dictate how you manage." (Mr. E. – Manufacturing)

660. "A person needs to be well-rounded and knowledgeable in several different areas. You need to become multi-faceted. Being merely single-faceted is unacceptable." (Mr. K. – Manufacturing)

LIFE LESSONS

As I told people about this book, some imagined that CEOs would dwell solely on business. But what these successful leaders most wanted to share are big-picture lessons about humanity, life, and bringing the whole of it together. Why is that? Because they understand that the principles of success and happiness are connected in every part of our being. Really, there are no boundaries between who we are and what we do. At least for the most successful people there are none. Compartmentalization doesn't fly.

17.   "Always, always, always treat everyone you ever meet as your equal. You are never better than anybody else, and no one is better than you." (Mr. D. – Business Services)

19.   "Be sure you're fair. Be fair to everyone you deal with, most importantly your employees and your clients. If you are fair to these people, you are setting yourself up for success. Employees will likely be more productive and your clients will remember you." (Mr. J. – Business Services)

26.   "In order to be successful, you have to always respect the people around you, and earn respect from them. From my experience I have learned that having respect from others, and vice versa, can simplify a lot of things and create a lot of extra opportunities. Having a network of people that are close and that respect you will bring you more benefit than harm.

Always put people first and try to build a long term rather than short term relationship with them. To be in a position of strategic management, one is always facing different kind of challenges. As a result, one will need help or advice from others too, and building a network of close relationships with other people always provides enormous benefits for your career." (Mr. D. – Financial Services)

59.   "Love people. We have people as customers, people as employees, people as suppliers, and people as shareholders. I find it impossible to believe that anyone could succeed in any role without this characteristic, although I see precious little emphasis given to it in business schools. I'm afraid that colleges do a good job of teaching concepts, but do nothing to instill the interpersonal skills that business demands. My selection process for promoting leaders is unique because it focuses heavily on the ability to create and cultivate genuine, caring relationships."   (Mr. H. – Manufacturing)

63.   "You should not become so focused on your work that you neglect your interests outside the office. This includes family, friends, hobbies, and even leisure time. I greatly values the time I spend with my family, and realize how important it is to maintain a proper balance between family and work. All too often individuals become so involved in one that the other is shunned, and more times than not it is the family that is neglected."   (Mr. G. – Transportation)

95.   "Having a life vision is a first step where many people mess up. This needs to include things such as: What do you want out of life? What do you want to

do with your life? Why did you pick this degree? Specifically, I recommend that you envision yourself at age 80. Where do you want to live? Do you want a $650,000 home, a good income, a good career? Do you want to coach little league baseball? It is not necessary to follow what everyone else is doing. And once you have determined your life plan, then make it happen. Create a plan, and then strategically manage that plan. Without a life vision though, nothing else matters; health and marital problems may follow. The more money one has, the less free time one will have given the increase in responsibilities that having money demands. Remember, your life decisions impact not only oneself, but also one's family and employees. In making a bad decision, both one's family and employees could be out in the cold." (Mr. P. – Financial Services)

115.   "Watch the news; be on top of what is going on in the world. This may help you make an important decision in the future. It will also help with intelligent conversation." (Mr. W. – Manufacturing)

118.   "My advice to you would be to stay focused on what you want in life. Always keep in mind where you're at, and where you want to be. You have to find a mission and or a purpose, something to strive for." (Mr. M. – Hospitality)

119.   "Think about this a lot: if you want to be successful in life, start thinking and planning now what you truly want to accomplish later." (Mr. K. – Hospitality)

122.   "Be very intentional about what you are doing. Stay focused. Get good coaching and go after good advice. Be dogmatic; it takes a while for good plans to mature. Sometimes you will not get what you set out for, and that is okay. You must be focused and intentional. If you are not, you will rarely get what you desire." (Mr. W. – Healthcare)

123.   "The first thing is to do a lot of research on you, and find your personality traits and God-given talent. We all can't be good at everything, so knowing yourself first is critical to be a good strategic manager. Once you find those things, find people that can help you maximize that strength. For example: my personality is the best at encouraging people. I want to be around the best encouragers in the world and learn from them how to encourage people. At the end of the day, my best success will be how I encouraged you to live up to your potential. You have to find out what makes you happy, and many of us spend a lot of our lives focusing on improving our weaknesses, and being things that people want us to be. And by the end of the day, we've wasted our strengths. Someday, God may ask the question 'How well did you do with the talents I gave you?' So I would sure like to know what those talents are. I think we shortchange ourselves on our happiness in life if we don't find those things. It's frustrating to be around people that don't utilize their talents, because they are usually unhappy. I think young people need to break down their strengths into three or four things they excel at. Then find a career and friends that share those strengths, because you can get energy from those people to be even better. For the things you aren't good at, you can find people to complement them, and hire them to do the things you

aren't very good at. If you can effectively use your talents, and employ others to complement your weaknesses, you can succeed anywhere." (Mr. B. – Real Estate)

126. "All great CEOs have one thing in common, great wills to succeed. You must never get discouraged. No matter what you deeply desire, you can achieve it. The only limitations you have in your life are ones that you have put into place." (Mr. J. – Information Technology)

131. "Success is something that you have to want to dedicate 100% of yourself to every day of the year. Naturally, most people don't really want to do that. It is okay to pursue your own ideas, but you must be fully committed to your actions and willing to face the consequences." (Mr. E. – Entertainment & Media)

133. "Students should not be setting goals to become CEOs or the richest people in the world. College students need to be setting goals of becoming a successful person in life. Becoming successful does not necessarily mean becoming the CEO of a Fortune 500 company. Becoming successful is the ability to be happy with what you are doing, and to be able to make a decent living with what you are doing." (Mr. S. – Healthcare)

157. "Know your limitations, but don't be limited by them. Be polite, and speak properly. Be straightforward and honest, even if it is unpleasant. Deliver on what you promise. Nobody cares about the reasons you failed, except your mother. Have a family

with whom you can share your life, personal and professional." (Mr. A. – Utilities)

159. "If you stand still, the horizon never changes. It is movement that creates opportunity, even if that movement is backwards. Another tip is that it's the smart, driven people who are willing to make sacrifices that make the truly great accomplishments. If you're not willing to give some things up, you will never make it big. Lastly, it's all about building relationships. You have to have integrity and be willing to make the effort to build good relationships. These will hold you up in your weak times and help you to shine in your strong times." (Mr. J. – Conglomerate)

172. "You should not define success in life as getting to the top ranked positions in an industry, or by how much you get paid. I define success as the constant pursuit of finding the right opportunities." (Mr. Z. – Energy, Mining & Materials)

185. "One must first understand themselves. It is very important to know your own strengths and weaknesses in order to capitalize on both. Always listen to people and their needs, and respect your differences. Never give up on yourself, but strive for excellence in every position. Prioritize to know what you want. When you know yourself and your priorities, you will know what you are willing to pay for things. Build upon this solid foundation to excel in all that you do. In the end, you must listen to your inner voice, have fun and keep things simple. It is a lot more fun to have a lot of money, but remain true to yourself and your family as you enjoy it." (Mr. H. – Transportation)

188. "Finally, always remember that there must be the proper balance of work and play." (Mr. G. – Conglomerate)

209. "Be unique; don't be afraid to be yourself. Stick to your guns, and be your own person. Be flexible. Continually learn. Be sure to learn a little about a lot." (Mr. V. – Food & Beverage)

216. "The worst of times are also the best of times. There's a big upside to the downside." (Mr. G. – Construction)

220. "When you're young you make a lot of mistakes and the only one that is hurt is you, so the pain is minimal. When you get married and make a mistake it affects two people, and then you have a child; now it affects someone your care about more than anything in the world, someone who has no way to handle it. So you get less and less willing to take on risk because of your personal life, if it goes traditionally. So you really want to make sure you are on a path you are going to enjoy because it does get a little more difficult to make those changes. You would hate to end up waking up one day retiring and saying those ten hours a day were horrible. So I would say pursue a passion, but while you are pursuing that passion stay open to new ideas. Continue to change, grow, and don't think you know it all." (Mr. Z. – Business Services)

223. "Make it clear to other people where you want to be. And most importantly, never stop dreaming. I still dream today, and no one can ever take away your dreams except for yourself." (Mr. H. – Hospitality)

225.   "When I was young, my thing was I wanted to get into the horse racing business. So I took my degree, and I went out and worked at a race track, and that turned out to be the best thing I ever did. I just kind of followed my dream. My dad had always told me, 'Follow your dream when you are young, or you are never going to follow it because you are going to get a family and commitments and this and that, and then you're not going to be able to do it.' So that would be my advice. If you have a special interest, just go do it even if you are sweeping floors so to speak; just start at the bottom. You will enjoy every minute of it if it's something you really like."   (Mr. T. – Consumer Products)

229.   "Have fun; life's too short to take things too seriously." (Mr. T. – Consumer Products)

231.   "Figure out how you as a person get persuaded and get things done. There are different types of personalities. You will have to get to know which one, or ones, you want to use and stick with that until they don't work anymore." (Mr. H. – Consumer Products)

234.   "Always accept information from others and invite ideas when planning. Be patient and understanding and tolerant of others, and don't expect too much too fast. Getting along with different personalities and having good people skills are the most important things." (Mr. R. – Financial Services)

235.   "Be true to yourself. Don't try to do it someone else's way; do it your way. Be playful with it. Be experimental. Take the chance. So have that sense of

going out and trying things; be more entrepreneurial, more experimental." (Dr. T. – Healthcare)

241.   "I would like to remind folks that you treat people the way you want to be treated, and don't step on a lot of toes on your way to the top because sometime you may see that same person on your way back down. If you bring people up with you, you'll be surprised how much wind you have at your back as you try to make it to the top." (Mr. S. – Retailing)

242.   "Read, read, and read some more. Have a thirst for information. You should read about whatever interests you. Whether you are intrigued by business, finance, management, product design, corporate culture, or people, just keep reading. If you read well-done biographies, you will learn a lot about people and different management styles."   (Mr. O. – Manufacturing)

244.   "Be positive and don't fall prey to negativity. It is a cancer. Nothing good can come from it." (Ms. C. – Manufacturing)

246.   "You've got to have a great attitude. People do not like to be around people who have a bad attitude. There's a book by Zig Ziglar called *Positive Mental Attitude.* It's a great book. It's probably old and everything else, but the idea, if you're not familiar with it, is that no one likes to be around someone who has a bad attitude. You actually have to train your mind to always be positive. One of the cool things that he had, and I actually took this thing from his book, is that when I woke up in the morning in my early twenties, I'd always say, 'God, I'm so tired.' That's the worst

way you can start your day. His thing is, as soon as you wake up when that alarm goes off, instead of thinking about how tired you are, the first thing you've got to say to yourself is, 'I'm going to have a great day.' He said to post your five goals on your mirror in the mornings where you brush your teeth, and I did that. Having a positive mental attitude goes a long way because no one wants to work with jerks. They also don't want to work around people who are negative. You know, you ask them how they're doing and they say, 'Uh, I'm alright.' Whether you're doing great or not doing great, people want to be around people who have a good attitude. Work hard and have a great attitude and you'll go far." (Mr. H. – Hospitality)

247.   "To be successful, you need to be okay with working outside of your comfort zone at any time. A CEO is a turtle on a fence; they didn't get there on their own. As soon as you find an opportunity, invest yourself into it 100%. If it doesn't work out for you, give yourself permission to change your path. Try as many experiences as you possibly can." (Mr. W. – Healthcare)

248.   "Never forget, you have a family along with a job." (Mr. G. – Utilities)

249.   "Some people get lucky. Some people get very lucky. But most successful people make their own breaks. This is done through hard work and self-confidence." (Mr. F. – Healthcare)

258.   "If you believe in what you want and go after it, you can accomplish whatever you put your mind to. You also need to have goals. You should never

compromise on what you want. Make goals both personally and within your company and make sure you accomplish them." (Ms. B. – Consumer Non-Products)

259. "Aspiration is another thing that is important. I think sometimes people don't have very high aspirations. You know, they are focused on doing the day-to-day responsibilities and their job; that's easy to have happen. But I think you have to set your standards higher; you'd better try to find ways how you can achieve that. Doing your job well is the foundation, but you have to build on it from there." (Mr. J. – Financial Services)

266. "Don't be greedy. Don't argue or fight over money." (Mr. Z. – Financial Services)

274. "Having balance in not only your work, but your personal and home life, makes all aspects of work more enjoyable, and most importantly keeps you focused on the large picture." (Mr. K. – Entertainment & Media)

287. "Don't only be motivated by things that are within your own best interest. Be mindful of this because it often doesn't come out until things go wrong. There is not a compensation plan that has ever been developed that works, and nobody thinks that they are over-compensated. I tell people that because it is the truth." (Mr. G. – Manufacturing)

288. "Choose your attitude. Choose your attitude. Focus on that every day." (Mr. H. – Hospitality)

290. "You have a choice: you can either be cynical, or you can be authentic. I urge you to choose to be authentic. It's easy to be cynical, but to be an effective strategic manager you need to be authentic." (Dr. M. – Healthcare)

293. "You have wonderful opportunities. The world out there. The world of business is so exciting, so challenging! You have tremendous opportunities. Anticipate, plan and prepare for it. It is exciting! And if you like it, it is great. All my days go by in a snap." (Mr. G. – Financial Services)

297. "Don't ever take yourself too seriously. That is something people on all levels need to remember. Try to enjoy what you do." (Mr. R. – Hospitality)

301. "Do you know what I'm proudest of right now? I'm proudest that I have 300 employees, and when they come to work they have an opportunity to provide for their family. I know this sounds corny and so cliched, but they have an opportunity to work in a safe environment, educate their children, and live a better life. That's what makes me proud. I'm one of the 300 and I'm part of that." (Mr. G. – Energy, Mining & Materials)

305. "Develop some empathy. If you can feel people's pain, that helps. Be gracious. It's not rocket science. All those things your mama taught you, she was right. She really was. There are times to be tough, and times to be not so tough. A good manager and a great leader has the innate ability to know the difference. It's the little things. I'll give you a perfect example. The 80 year-old customer that I was working

with yesterday on her checking account, I was struggling with that for a day or two, and I went to Bookkeeping yesterday, and said, 'Someone's got to help me here.' So we sat down and looked at it, and two or three of the girls came around and helped. Then all of a sudden it was like it jumped off the page at us, and we knew what the problem was. I walked out of the bank yesterday and said, 'Pizza is on me tomorrow. Y'all order pizza, and I'm paying.' You would have thought that I had given them all a thousand dollar raise because they were so happy. So be kind to people; be nice to people. 'Yes ma'am, no ma'am,' all those things Mama taught you. It's true in the business world. People will say you can't be that way; you've got to be tough; you've got to put this face on in front of everyone. I don't think so, not in my world, not where I reside. I want to reside somewhere people care about me and I care about them, and it's sincere. So be sincere; be authentic; don't try to be somebody you're not. People can see through that so quickly; they know when you're being fake. Be who you are." (Mr. B. – Financial Services)

308. "Set personal goals, just like a business establishes goals. Have short-term and long-term plans. Communicate those with your spouse, and make changes to those plans when life throws you curve balls. I think a lot of young people with college degrees don't have a plan other than to get a job, pay for a car and place to stay, and beer money; everything else is happenstance – no planning for children, the children's education, their own retirement. They just kept taking out bigger mortgages to pay for more stuff. I wish we could help them learn that early in life so they all had a chance to better the next generation like my parents

did for me and your grandparents did for your parents. Sounds more like a parent than a CEO, doesn't it?" (Dr. H. – Food & Agriculture)

312. "If there is anything that I have learned, I would tell you that individual human beings – not only individuals but also groups of human beings – have tremendous capacity to do things with their minds and the capabilities. The tools that exist today are amazing; don't underestimate that. Don't ever underestimate it. Thinking back to my parents' or grandparents' era, you know they didn't have nearly the tools, but the things they accomplished were incredible. Here we have all these tools and access – information, media, communications, technology – it's just wonderful, and sometimes it's overwhelming. But in the end it takes human beings to do all that, so I tell people never to forget that." (Mr. V. – Consumer Products)

320. "You have to be open-minded, and you always need a positive attitude no matter how tough it seems to be. Just keep a healthy attitude. Always stay positive." (Mr. G. – Manufacturing)

322. "Understand that the only way to be successful is by helping someone else be successful. The strategy is to create win-win opportunities, make money and have fun." (Mr. C. – Food & Agriculture)

324. "Don't ever be late! I can't stress that enough. I always went with the motto, 'Early is on time; on time is late.'" (Mr. S. – Financial Services)

333. "You should be able to be an avid listener, but also not just wait for your turn to talk." (Mr. E. – Healthcare)

336. "I have the following rule for being successful: Use please and thank you. I don't care whether you are at the top or the bottom, use those words. A little kindness and respect can go a long way to making friends and progress." (Mr. K. – Manufacturing)

337. "People who don't dream big enough are the ones who hit a plateau at some point and too soon get where they didn't want to be. Always ask yourself, 'Where do I want to be in five years, and what do I need do to get there?'" (Mr. T. – Information Technology)

338. "I think it's a huge, wide, fantastic world out there. For those who wish to stand up and take advantage of it, you are going to have a wonderful, wonderful life. For those of your peers who think they are entitled to everything, they are going to have a difficult time. Nowadays, the world is offering far more opportunity, but in conjunction with that it is becoming much more competitive. You have to have passion for what you do and perseverance for what you do, then you have to throw in a little serendipity. Those who think they will be handed things need to be careful." (Mr. S. – Financial Services)

339. "We are in control of our emotions; people can't hurt you unless you let them." (Ms. H. – Financial Services)

340. "Be upbeat; nothing takes place of a great personality. Be persistent, determined, patient, and have a sense of humor." (Mr. G. – Construction)

341. "Responsible means you are 'response-able.' So if you say, 'Well this is the way I am; it's just the way I was raised, and I am making this decision because I have always done it this way,' well excuse me, you are not acting 'response-able.' You should have enough brain power to say, 'Stop; forget what the status quo is.' Think about this. It's kind of like people say, and this is an extreme example, 'I can't quit smoking.' Well you know what? If you want to quit smoking, quit smoking. People who quit smoking make a decision they aren't going to do it anymore. And when the gain of the result outweighs the vice, you will stop doing it. So where am I going? What I am really telling you is to take responsibility for yourself and what you do. Don't blame other people, and don't make excuses. You are able to do whatever you choose to do. And if you aren't able because you don't possess the skill or knowledge, then you have got to go get the skill or knowledge." (Mr. D. – Retailing)

353. "Every individual needs to know him or herself before they can expect to be successful." (Mr. K. – Consumer Services)

375. "I would say the first thing is you need to learn is to know yourself as well as you possibly can. There's all kinds of different types of assessments, and I recommend doing as many of them as possible because you really do need to know yourself. That will help you in your interactions at all levels." (Mr. H. – Manufacturing)

385. "Always seek the truth. And when you find it, get on the side of truth. There's nothing worse than trying to argue from the side you know is flawed and wrong. The truth will always win out in the end. That theme has played out over and over and over in my career. It may be costly; it may be expensive; it may be tempting to bull your way over people: 'I can win; I can overpower like poker players who put all their chips in.' But clearly, that is merely a short-term strategy. You really have to proactively seek out the truth. When you do that, people over time will follow you because they want to be on the correct side. If you speak the truth, people will migrate to you and your position. It only makes sense." (Mr. R. – Construction)

395. "Doing a personal SWOT analysis can also be beneficial for your own good. It can help you find your own strengths, weaknesses, opportunities, and threats and help you develop yourself." (Mr. S. – Manufacturing)

396. "The world is asleep. Stay awake. People are awake and they go sleep, and when they wake up, they wake up to the nightmare. They don't like the nightmare, so they go back to sleep. But sooner or later we all have to deal with the nightmare of reality. I know that and you know that. Don't let it get you down. When you find people that are staying awake, and they are true to their word, and they don't cause any troubles, hire them, embrace them, and don't let them out of your life." (Mr. S. – Hospitality)

398. "You must learn to be still. Don't buy into any one thing you hear. Don't buy into one set of beliefs; you must remain open. Be patient; it will come to you.

It takes time. The best new employees come in open-minded with not a lot of preconceived notions; they listen. Sit back; be patient and listen. There are usually reasons why people – especially older more experienced people – do things. Try to understand that before you try to change things." (Mr. R. – Consumer Products)

401. "A word of advice I would give you is to know basic grammar and basic math. We have seen the entrance of portfolios in the education curriculum while the department dropped the requirement for students to memorize multiplication tables. Believe it or not, we do see people when they take pre-employment tests who can't tell you what 25% of 80 is. They just don't understand how to do it. That is a problem." (Mr. M. – Energy, Mining & Materials)

405. "I am going to tell you the same thing I told my daughters. The first thing is to learn finance. If you can't read a balance statement, or a profit/loss statement, then you can't perform your job as a CEO. That is a critical thing. It's going to serve you well in your home and it's going to serve you well in your business. Be very disciplined in your own personal financial life. If you can't be disciplined with your own personal finances, you're not going to be disciplined with your own business' finances." (Mr. B. – Food & Agriculture)

408. "Don't worry that you're pestering someone. I can look at our most successful people around here; they're the ones who pester everybody. Now, obviously you can take it to an extreme. But this theme of the squeaky wheel, those are the ones that are the

most successful. You've got to be a squeaky wheel. I think it's that extra element – putting yourself in position to be recognized, and backing it up with substance. It's that intangible – not being afraid to ask questions, not being afraid to call. You weren't afraid to call; that's why you called me; that's why you emailed me. Don't ever be afraid to ask. Don't ever be afraid to ask." (Mr. T. – Financial Services)

408.   "I'm a big believer in thank you notes – hand-written thank you notes. I know all the young people who have written me a hand-written thank you note. If you mention somebody's name, I can tell you that person wrote me a hand-written thank you note. It just shows me an extra effort." (Mr. T. – Financial Services)

414.   "It goes a long way in your life to have things you really care about in life. For me, it is my family, my friends, and this business. I started in with a few guys, and we didn't really know how it would work. But we planned long and hard before we started; we've worked really hard, and we never looked back. We aren't out of the woods yet, but I am already proud of what we have accomplished. So just remember that no matter where you end up in life, be doing something you take pride in and treat it like that." (Mr. M. – Healthcare)

416.   "Be about the long-term, and always ask the question, 'Am I moving forward?' If you are not moving forward, you are moving backward. Innovate or perish." (Mr. B. – Business Services)

417.   "Go out into the world and live; enjoy experiences, and learn by doing." (Mr. M. – Manufacturing)

424.   "Understand your spouse. If things are not right at home, they will not be right at work. And if they are not right at work, then they will not be right at home. Each one requires one hundred percent effort to be successful." (Mr. B. – Construction)

428.   "You also must have a vision. It does not have to be monetary goals. If early on you can develop a vision of personal success, make sure you do what is important to you. You should write it down and have goals that you review. It is more than money and building an organization; it is more about having a balanced life. Find what makes you happy and something you can tell yourself that you're proud of." (Mr. C. – Business Services)

433.   "The world is constantly changing, so you have to find ways to differentiate yourself. You have to know what value you add. Do that by asking, 'What is the biggest thing that I personally can add value to?' There is a whole bunch of things that I have to do every day. Some of them are a top priority, but then with some of them for example, I have to sit back and figure out what my purpose at a meeting is. 'What value am I? Am I a participant, the leader, the decision-maker? What value am I adding? What responsibility am I adding?' When you figure out those questions, you will know what differentiates you from others." (Ms. T. – Consumer Products)

435.   "Sit down and think about what your vision for yourself is, right down to your own personal level. What's important to you? You need a vision, mission, and principles. Ask yourself, 'Where do I see myself? How am I going to get there? What am I doing day-to-day, and how am I going to do it?' I just reacted to things for too long. You need to know what you want, and then go get it. The earlier that you can figure out your vision, the better of you will be, and don't be afraid to try stuff at the same time. If you don't know what you want to be, then try a couple things and see from there. Don't lose your balance or your priorities. My priorities are God, family, career. I asked my father if he ever regretted getting off the corporate ladder, and he said, 'Are you kidding?' So what that he made a little less money; it wasn't worth losing his family." (Mr. H. – Utilities)

441.   "My   instinct   is   to   follow   opportunity. Sometimes there are not opportunities that are easy to detect. Therefore you end up making your own opportunities." (Mr. B. – Energy, Mining & Materials)

444.   "I think that principles of personal finance are so important. My wife says that it is four things: unsecured debt is bad; saving is good; giving is fun, and stuff is meaningless. If you'll live that way in your life, in your marriage, in your future business, then you'll always do well. I would tell you to trade stuff for experiences. You might want to take a year and go work in India at a school – a slum school – or go on an international justice mission and try to free child slaves in some country. Don't trade into stuff; don't trade into cars, apartments and houses – all the junk of the world. But trade into experiences; you'll like those

a lot more for a lot longer time. Healthy experiences will bring great gain. There's plenty of time to make money later." (Mr. C. – Financial Services)

445. "Don't stress so much. My son started working for the company a few years ago, and I just put him in charge of our secondary market. With this bigger leadership position, he has stayed tense and worried about his decisions. It is hard to tell yourself not to stress, but you have to learn how to do it. I used to go home from work stressed out almost every night, and my wife told me I needed to stop bringing the stresses with me. I decided to try to do something about it, so I read everything I could about how to relieve stress and better cope with it. It has taken me about five years to get to the point that I am at today, and I am fairly laid back now. I read a lot and that is what I suggest you should do. I've told my son that he should do the same thing because stress only makes your decisions harder and is a burden on your life. You have to learn to relax and take each day at a time. The quicker you can discover how to deal with your stress, the better off you will be in your career." (Mr. R. – Financial Services)

460. "The most important piece of advice I can give you would be to do your best and always be thinking about how to apply what you have learned to better yourself." (Mr. T. – Construction)

462. "You might be a little bit surprised by this answer, but it starts by staring into the mirror and figuring out who you are. Most people wander through life in a manner that's very similar to getting into your car in the driveway and backing out without

any idea where the destination is. We should get everybody to write their obituary before they graduate from college because it forces humans to confront the one thing they don't want to face – mortality. Force them to look backwards and say, 'My life is over; what has it amounted to?' That would force people into the strategic management of themselves. The insights that would flow from that would be of immense value in answering life's questions. Unfortunately, very few people ever do that – go to the end and look backward. But if you think about it, when you get in your car and drive off the lot, you'll know exactly where you're going. And you probably have a pretty good idea of what it's going to look like when you get there. Why we don't go through life like that is a bit of a mystery. But I definitely believe in creating life strategies." (Mr. B. – Consumer Products)

474. "Be completely, totally, utterly, always dissatisfied. If you are constantly looking for ways to improve, and are never satisfied, then you are never complacent. Everything can be improved." (Mr. S. – Manufacturing)

482. "Everybody wants to be in a glorious place someday, but a lot of times you have to go through a lot to get to the top. So there's tough days ahead to get there; everything doesn't just fall into place. There are hills and valleys. But what I have found to be true over time is that you don't grow on that hilltop. If you look over a mountain range, at the very top you don't see many trees; trees can't grow at the top of that mountain very often. It's always down in the valley that you see trees growing. That has a lot to do with

life. If we're always on top, we quit learning. It is down in the valley – in those tough times when you get knocked down – that you learn how to grow again, and then you can climb back up to the mountain." (Mr. E. – Manufacturing)

484.   "You will have to go right through the good and the bad, so don't get too caught in the highs and the lows. It is not as good or bad as people think. Know what you are trying to do and you will get through. How you judge success, someone else won't. It is not about money because there is never enough." (Mr. H. – Healthcare)

491.   "Never lose your edge or your mentality; stay driven. Be thick-skinned, completely open to criticism. Be willing to accept disappointment, but make sure you come back with resilience." (Mr. S. – Construction)

501.   "Everyone is going to have difficult days. Some days are just going to beat you up. Just don't do anything rash. Go to bed, get up, and start over tomorrow. Live today and do the right things. Know where you want to end up, and just put one foot in front of the other, and let nothing get in your way." (Mr. H. – Manufacturing)

504.   "First of all I would get out in the real world a little bit before you get a job. Don't worry so much about your career. Going from college straight to your job means you are there for the rest of your life, so go out and do something you enjoy." (Mr. H. – Manufacturing)

506. "First and foremost, stay positive. People will always put roadblocks in your path, but you must remember you can overcome them. Something I wish someone had really stressed to me was to not get discouraged and not let the little things bring you down. And lastly, really appreciate all the things that you have, and remember that there is good all around." (Mr. H. – Financial Services)

507. "I think people getting started today really need to be very selective, not only in choosing their profession but also whom they are associated with. Understanding yourself and what motivates you is so important, not only in what we do for a living, but who we partner with in marriage, religion, and education. All of our being is structured by who we come in contact with, and the people who have influenced us. I think we have to be aware how those influences influence us because we are constantly changing. I don't believe in the same things I believed 20 years ago because my experiences changed me." (Mr. M. – Food & Agriculture)

512. "You have to find that personal balance outside of work so you have something that allows you to let off steam. I have found that most CEOs today have a hobby – whether it is wood working, music, etc. – that uses the artistic side of the brain." (Mr. E. – Manufacturing)

518. "The best quality that you can have as a person, I think, is vulnerability – being authentic about who you are." (Ms. K. – Consumer Services)

520. "Understand the value of respect, humility, and courtesy. Understanding these factors will get you far in any industry you venture into. Treat every individual you come into contact with the same respect. This reflects greatly upon yourself as an individual as well as your business. People recognize these traits and will hold you in high esteem because of them." (Mr. B. – Manufacturing)

521. "Life is what you make of it. I would ask, what do you want? Money's just... it's not that important. Its really not that important. It doesn't make you happy. That cliché is so true. I look back at making 50 grand a year, and many times that now. I was just as happy poor when I was 28 with my wife I had two kids and bought my first house – an $80,000 dollar home, I frickin' loved it. You know, a little three bedroom ranch with cracks in the walls, whatever. (chuckles) I was just as happy then as I am now that I have anything I want. I've got a plane and a golf course – you're no happier. So it's not about the money; it's taking pride in what you do. The money is just a barometer to tell you how well you're doing, to me. It has more to do with pride and winning, and satisfaction in your efforts and having success, than it is chasing the almighty dollar. It's true. That VW Touareg is mine. It could be a Mercedes; I don't really care. I drive a Volkswagen; I like it. That stuff is just meaningless as you get older. And I guess you have to get to that point where you finally start making money and you go, 'You know what? It wasn't the money that motivated me. I liked being in the game and winning the game.' You know? And being proud – being proud of your accomplishments, etc. – that's way more important than material things that you think are

gonna make you happy someday down the road. They never do. They never do. Clichés; but all very true." (Mr. O. – Hospitality)

522. "I am the lucky one; there is nothing else you could ask me to be. I am a very happy person; I am making a difference. The reason I know that is because I am spiritually strong, and you have to be too. Whatever your faith is, be conscious of that and allow God to speak into your life, your world, your spirit and be strong. Know what God is asking you to do and go do it. Do it with passion, hard work, and with everything you've got, and you will be a happy and successful person. If you live a life of bitterness and unforgiveness, you might be right, but you will be miserable." (Mr. M. – Food & Agriculture)

524. "Follow your heart, but understand that your journey will be messy. Be flexible, and never be afraid to take action. Always remember that every experience is a good one in one way or another. Do your best to approach the right direction aggressively. People who know what they want in life tend to handle the ups and downs better than those who do not. So never lose sight of what means the most to you. Sometimes it is easy to forget about what truly matters most to us. Do not let those things slip away because you are too focused on other things." (Mr. M. – Manufacturing)

528. "The most important thing is being at peace. If you are at peace, everything falls into place. Hopefully, when you reach a certain point in life, you find peace." (Mr. C. – Financial Services)

530. "Work hard, play hard; treat people fairly, and do what's right. Don't take yourself too seriously. Never quit learning. Don't try to be president on the first day, but be the best you can be even in menial, entry-level positions. Surround yourself with good, smart people. Trust people. Show integrity. Remember who pays you. Have fun. Consider the banker. Give the banker opportunities, and give him a voice; they will respect you if you do this. Show empathy. And spend plenty of time with your friends and family." (Mr. B. – Financial Services)

532. "Be solid. You have to climb the ladder and prove you can do the work. Have your priorities in order and have good solid values. Get your education. Use common sense. Be an honest worker. Give the company eight full hours. Say, 'I am glad to go to work.' Have an eye of a tiger. Look for and conquer challenges. Follow your dreams. Always go to the next level. Love what you do." (Mr. T. – Conglomerate)

543. "Once you start your career, make sure you are able to be involved with the community that you work in." (Mr. M. – Healthcare)

544. "First, let others talk so you can see what they have experienced. Learn from their experiences. Take away thoughts that are interesting to you from their stories. Allow what they tell you to make you think. Open yourself up to learn something new everyday. Although it's tough for some people, challenge yourself to learn, mingle and make new friends whenever given the opportunity. Respect people's opinions. If you respect people, you will get respect in return. You never know what connections you may

make and how those connections may change your life." (Mr. F. – Financial Services)

552.   "One of the most important things is to not keep score with dollars and cents. What I mean by this is that you should not constantly be comparing yourself with those people who have the biggest houses, or who drive the nicest cars because in most cases those people are not truly happy. Many would say that they are successful; however I tend to judge success in a different manner. I think that some of the most successful people in the world can be policemen, teachers, whatever, so long as they are happy with what they do. You need to have the courage and conviction to do what you want to do and not what others want you to do. Also, make sure that you recognize that there are very few fatal mistakes, provided that they do not deal with a moral perspective or your integrity. Many successful people in this world find what they love to do most and they take a shot. They have the courage and conviction to try something unique because it is what they wanted to do and not what others were telling them to do." (Mr. B. – Food & Agriculture)

555.   "I have been with this company for 40 years, and my time has gone by quickly. But it is important to remember that you have a life outside of work, so you must find time for all aspects of your life. I have to spend time coaching, motivating, mentoring, counseling, as well as time for board meetings on acquisitions, teleconferences too. But all of these things would not be possible if I were not in a position of mental and physical health." (Mr. W. – Consumer Products)

556. "If you are not confident in your abilities, others will sense that and things will become hard for you. Be confident; be worthy of being trusted; be who you are, and I have no doubt you will succeed. You can't expect anybody to give it to you; there is too much of that out there now." (Mr. N. – Energy, Mining & Materials)

558. "The next 30 years are going to fly by faster than you realize. For an intelligent, self-motivated, and productive person, time is a very precious commodity. Remember to balance your life with regard to your family, your emotional and spiritual health, your physical health, your professional career, and your future intellectual and creative activities. You will not regret doing so. But it is very easy to let professional endeavors hoard most of your time. Again, you only have a limited amount of time in each of your days, weeks, years, and your lifetime." (Mr. H. – Transportation)

565. "Keep it simple. My favorite quotation from Leonardo Da Vinci is, 'Simplicity is the ultimate sophistication.' In this day and age, we try to make things more complicated than they really are, particularly with access to information. Don't make things complicated." (Mr. S. – Food & Agriculture)

667. "Most importantly, if you are not happy with your life, your business will suffer." (Mr. S. – Financial Services)

MENTORS

Note that a relationship with a "natural" mentor – as opposed to an assignment with a "manufactured" one – is much more effective for both parties involved. Strive to make it a two-way street. The more you put in, the more you get out. And note that having a good mentor is all about changing your self, about learning and growing in ways that you would not do on your own.

2.   "You can't be told what to understand; management is self-taught. A mentor cannot simply tell you what you need to know in order to be a strategic manager; you must open your eyes and see how things work in situations. I will remember my experiences in life; I will not remember what someone told me I should know." (Mr. L. – Healthcare)

56.   "Align yourself with successful people and learn from them. You need to get with people who are good mentors. They will open doors and new perspectives for you, and provide you with otherwise unavailable opportunities and challenges. You can learn a lot from them, especially on how and what makes the company really work – a perspective of the whole." (Mr. R. – Manufacturing)

57.   "Find someone you respect, both in and out of the office, and emulate them. Notice how they interact with people, how they make decisions, and how they manage crises. Emulate those aspects that make you respect them so highly, and learn to act differently than

those you do not agree with." (Mr. D. – Manufacturing)

71.   "Unfortunately one cannot find a blueprint that will clearly and concisely explain the appropriate action for any given situation. There are certain nuances of management than can only be learned firsthand and cannot be taught in any book. So I strongly recommended having a mentor. Oftentimes the only way someone in your shoes can learn the nuances of strategic management is to do so firsthand. Watching excellent leaders respond to difficult situations is perhaps the most valuable source of information anyone could ever receive." (Mr. T. – Hospitality)

77.   "The best way to learn how a business really works is to adopt a mentor, someone whom you can trust and will give sound advice on the ways of the world. This is the best way to learn what makes people tick. Mentors are invaluable concerning your growth as an employee. But also, note that you learn from a mentor so you as an employee can create your own way of doing things. Emulating your mentor is not the way to go." (Mr. R. – Financial Services)

115.   "Always look ahead at leaders on top of you analyze their strengths and weakness critique them. Look at the decisions they make and think how you would make that decision." (Mr. W. – Manufacturing)

235.   "Find good mentors. Too often young people don't have the gift and benefit of good mentors and people that are willing to help them. The academic and the theoretical in the classroom is all important,

but what you learn from mentors is what they have applied. They know what works and doesn't work and how to avoid making a lot of the mistakes because they have made them." (Dr. T. – Healthcare)

255. "Learn the culture of the company; immerse yourself in it and be a part of it. Look for people that can be a mentor to you, and maybe have more than one. Take two fields you are interested in, find two mentors, and go from there. Look for the best performers when choosing mentors, study them and combine their ways to become a better worker." (Mr. H. – Construction)

256. "Being young, there are always those people out in the world that are looking out for you to give a helping hand." (Mr. G. – Construction)

272. "Wherever you have the opportunity to find a mentor, take full advantage! Ask them for something. Be hungry for knowledge!" (Dr. H. – Business Services)

283. "Really look for individuals if you can. Who's going to be my boss? Who's going to be my mentor? Who will take me under his or her wing and help me develop as an individual? I was fortunate enough when I joined my family's business that I could almost pick the company I worked for in terms of a training program. But I really picked an individual. That was a really good decision as I look back. It's not just the organization, but if you can, pick the individual." (Mr. S. – Entertainment & Media)

296. "Obviously you are going to have to have a mentor along the way. That doesn't change from 40

years ago. You've got to be able to accept constructive criticism and be able to change directions if need be." (Mr. H. – Financial Services)

320. "You should look for a mentor – somebody who has knowledge, experience, and is willing to take you under his wing. Somebody like that is hard to find, but they are out there. If you find one, listen to him. Listen closely to what he says, and follow that. Finding a good mentor is almost as important as good education." (Mr. G. – Manufacturing)

334. "Find a mentor! Some companies have formal mentoring programs; at most places generally it is informal. Regardless, find a mentor. Be careful about the selection of that mentor. They need to be somebody that has accomplished many of the goals that you have set for yourself." (Mr. S. – Information Technology)

355. "I want to urge you to find a mentor. Be intentional about getting a mentor because a mentor will help you to operate at a higher level sooner. Gain his wisdom as well as his knowledge." (Mr. K. – Energy, Mining & Materials)

365. "I've had a lot of good mentors, and I've had some bad ones. So I have tried to learn from the good ones, and understand that this is not what I would want as an employee to have a boss from among the bad ones. I've tried to learn from the good and bad, and hopefully mold my style based on that." (Mr. M. – Utilities)

377.   "You have to listen, and you have to find ways to listen. When you get ready in the morning what is one of the last things you do? You look at the mirror and check your hair, tie, or just your appearance in general before you leave your house. You have to find people that can be that mirror for you in life." (Mr. D. – Retailing)

395.   "One thing students can do is cultivate a mentor. A mentor can help teach a young person different aspects of business that they may not be able to learn in a classroom setting. For instance, young business professionals who are fresh from college will need to learn proper business etiquette – from how to dress to actions in the workplace." (Mr. S. – Manufacturing)

406.   "Try to learn every chance you get. You will find all kind of managers and successful people who are willing to help you. Seek help from people that you want to be like. Be willing to ask for help to help you advance." (Mr. H. – Entertainment & Media)

420.   "I would recommend individuals seek out and identify a mentor. You or your employer could identify someone to guide you through the new adventures of a career. If that is not accessible, then I would be careful to watch other people in the work setting. Personally, I have worked for and been around a lot of really good people. I believe my style is a collection of what I've seen around me over time, and deciding for myself what I like and what I didn't – what worked and what did not work." (Mr. M. – Consumer Services)

433. "You can also seek people who are very well thought of in the organization, and ask them if they would mentor you. I have been so fortunate to work with some of the best and brightest as my mentors, and have learned invaluable information that has helped me tremendously in my career." (Ms. T – Consumer Products)

450. "Without a doubt, in anyone's career, you need to be sure to have an experienced mentor. I think it's very important to have a mentor. If you have a mentor, they will help bring a level of experience, knowledge, ideas, counsel, advice, and a pat on the back. A mentor will help you through, and will become your confidant." (Ms. B. – Food & Agriculture)

490. "Find somebody like me to be your boss, that will take an interest in you and will protect you in a corporate area because if you're really smart and really sharp, you will find that people will compete with you and occasionally try to cut your legs out from under you. My biggest advice is hopefully you will find a supervisor who takes a sincere interest in you and wants to see you develop and grow. Finding a good supervisor is more important than earning a lot of money starting out, I think in all honesty, because they will teach you things you need to do and how to do it. You'll get out of school and you'll know that you are really smart. But you're smart in the books. You're not smart in the way a company runs and the politics that go on in that company. You need to find a good boss. If you can find a good boss that will be sincere and care about you, that's worth a couple thousand dollars because they will teach you the right things to do, and they'll protect you." (Mr. R. – Healthcare)

491.   "Take advantage in your young career to seek as much advice as possible. Find a mentor, someone within your company who can bring you up to speed and tell you, 'This is how it is done; this is what we expect.' That's the thing about young people with new ideas – you have the potential to step into a long-standing company and offer a whole new perspective that has never been proposed because of the new learning techniques you have been exposed to. Fresh, new ideas combined with the experience of a mentor can take you, as well as the company, a long way." (Mr. S. – Construction)

498.   "Get the support of your supervisor; get a mentor – one or two in your organization. Maybe not even in your organization, maybe in another organization. I think that is very helpful. Find someone that is about five years ahead of you, and talk to them about how they got where they are. Then be very open to change." (Mr. M. – Manufacturing)

550.   "Be resourceful enough to seek out a mentor at each stage of your career. Allowing yourself to be guided by someone with more experience or wisdom will not only provide you with a positive role model, but will also keep you humble and realistic as you aspire toward your goals." (Mr. T. – Consumer Services)

551.   "I would never want you to be anybody other than who you are, but if you see somebody that you admire and think, 'I like the way he thinks; I like the way he talks; I like the way he carries himself; I would like to know more,' hook yourself up with those mentors. Learn as much as you can." (Mr. R. – Financial Services)

567. "You want to work for organizations that you respect and like, that have expertise, and you know you're going to learn from. More importantly, really look for individuals if you can. 'Who's going to be my boss? Who's going to be my mentor? Who will take me under his or her wing and help me develop as an individual?' It's not just the organization, but the individual." (Mr. S. – Entertainment & Media)

MISTAKES AND FAILURE

Our failings get us in trouble only if we knew better, if we do not own up to them, or if we resist changing our behaviors. If we knew better than to do something wrong, it is not a "mistake;" it is a failure of character. People will tend to be lenient and forgiving to the degree that we admit our wrongs and strive to change.

10.   "Being a good manager means that you have to be able to accept that you will be wrong some of the time and then learn from those mistakes. Sometimes there is not a perfect answer to a problem." (Mr. S. – Food & Agriculture)

16.   "You cannot let failure slow you down; failure is going to happen no matter what. Managers have to get up, reflect on why a decision was a failure, and try again. No one has been successful at everything they have done." (Mr. T. – Business Services)

39.   "It is important to be able to admit when a poor decision has been made. If you admit your failure quickly, damage will be held to a minimum and there will still be opportunity to correct it. Once the bad decision is out of control, you are no longer able to fix it, but instead can only go into 'salvage mode' to try and keep the damage minimized as much as possible. Excellent managers develop a disciplined process they use when addressing bad decisions." (Mr. B. – Energy, Mining & Materials)

60. "Eliminate fear. Most uncertainty that any business leader faces is internal and illusionary, because we are afraid of failure. I try to instill in my employees that there is no real competition out there, that any problems created by competition or the environment are simply reflections of failures internal to the organization. In failure, the biggest problem is us. Fear is a terrible motivator because it compels action to reduce the fear rather than actions that are truly best for the company. If leaders can eliminate fear, they can focus on opportunities and threats as they truly are, not as they have been distorted to be." (Mr. C. – Financial Services)

66. "Always accept responsibility for your actions – good and bad. If you make a mistake, admit it, then fix it and move on. Do not make excuses or try to cover it up." (Mr. F. – Financial Services)

116. "Follow through. Young and ambitious employees get wonderful ideas that can really boost the profitability of their firm, but they too often fail to see the project all the way through. Nothing can be learned of success or failure if you don't see it through and thoroughly evaluate the results. Then, always be ready and eager to change direction." (Mr. Z. – Financial Services)

118. "You should be able to learn from your mistakes, because what learning takes sometimes is having some humility." (Mr. M. – Hospitality)

124. "Mistakes and experience are the same. Everything we do is part of the learning process,

whether the experience is good or bad." (Mr. K. – Retailing)

125. "You must learn from failures and not dwell on the past. Early in my career I made many mistakes that I will not make today because I lived through them. They made me stronger, and now I know how to handle those situations. I believe that if you take every mistake as being a horrible setback to success, then you will miss out on great learning opportunities." (Mr. H. – Energy, Mining & Materials)

235. "You can't be afraid to make mistakes. If you are genuinely trying to do the right thing, and you genuinely know who you are, then you have to put yourself out there and be able to make those mistakes. Fear will cause you to miss out on a lot of opportunities." (Dr. T. – Healthcare)

246. "Don't tolerate excuses and failures; just don't accept it. It's going to happen. You're going to get fired. You're going to have setbacks. But I have friends who aren't where they want to be, and they blame everyone but themselves." (Mr. H. – Hospitality)

253. "There is no shame in failing. There is shame in failing to try. Most creative breakthroughs occur when your back is against the wall." (Mr. H. – Manufacturing)

268. "Do not be afraid to fail. Do not be afraid to try something new. Most people and businesses fail at some point, the only way you're going to learn is if you try. That one idea that you thought might not work might open a million doors for you." (Mr. J. – Manufacturing)

292.   "The best advice I can give is to learn from your mistakes. As a leader, I have made decisions that proved to be wrong ones down the road, but I reflected on why those decisions were made and what went differently from how we thought it would go. Once a lesson has been learned from your mistakes, admit the decision was wrong, explain how the decision was made, and what should have been done in its place. Then move on better for the experience." (Mr. S. – Business Services)

323.   "Don't be afraid to screw up and make mistakes. It's much easier and better to do it early on, to get out of a mistake early in your career. If you are 40 or 50 years old and you're a CEO and you screw up, your ass will be gone. When you're 25, people will laugh and tell you to chalk it up as a learning experience." (Mr. J. – Construction)

354.   "Don't expect to be an overnight success. Failure is a part of life, and everyone needs to fail a time or two so you know what being at the bottom feels like. There isn't a better way of learning about something then failing at it." (Mr. M. – Hospitality)

413.   "Make bad decisions good ones. Your success is determined by how you handle your failures – and you will have many. Know that in the long run everything happens for a reason. Don't let something that happens that you don't think you can deal with get you down. Pull up your bootstraps and deal with it. Give every opportunity that you have everything that you can give it. It can better you. If you are constantly bettering yourself, it will take you where you need to go." (Ms. W. – Consumer Products)

426. "Some people ride in sinking ships. Try to visualize a sinking ship and picture one person bailing water from the ship with a bucket. They will fail. But if that person is you, that's okay because you have another life; you have to try again. Times will get tough, but you must not give up because of failure. If you are persistent, you will eventually succeed. More than anything, don't quit. Failure is acceptable, but quitting is not. Be sure and do the best job you can at any task, and if you fail you will still be able to sleep at night." (Mr. C – Energy, Mining & Materials)

428. "Be willing to admit and learn from mistakes. Understand that rarely if ever are mistakes fatal. Learn from success too. You can go from failure to success in days, and vice versa. Every obstacle is an opportunity." (Mr. C. – Business Services)

500. "Be more creative than predictable. Fail fast and fail cheap; just let go of failed ideas. Failure is a tool for learning, so don't be scared or discouraged to take risk." (Mr. H. – Entertainment & Media)

523. "Never underestimate the value of the mistakes that are going to be made, and what you do with those mistakes and how you address those challenges. Allowing for risk-taking and mistakes, and how you react to those mistakes, is really the biggest judge, to me, of a leader – how that leader responds to opportunities and challenges, and how they manage their people to accomplish the mission and vision of the organization." (Mr. K. – Food & Agriculture)

539. "When you get knocked down, always get up, keep fighting, and keep trying. The bottom line is that

you are not going to bat 1,000. When you get knocked down, always dust yourself off and give it another try. I say this because we've failed too. Things don't last forever; things are not always going to be a success right off the bat. We've been very successful in being able to cut out when we recognize a failure and move on. And we've been very successful in being able to take several concepts and turn them into extremely profitable business opportunities." (Mr. M. – Hospitality)

551. "Remember the mistakes you make. Don't dwell on them, but don't forget them because that is how you learn to get better. There was an IBMer who made a decision and he lost IBM one million dollars. When he went in to tell the boss, he knew for sure that his boss was going to tell him he had been fired. In fact, his boss said, 'You know what? I am not going to fire you because I think we just spent a million dollars training you on how to never make that mistake again. I have got faith in you, so don't make that mistake again.' I get asked a lot, 'What things have you done well? Talk about those. And tell me about some things you haven't done well.' My advice to you – what I try to do – is: Try to learn from our mistakes; just don't make them again, but remember them. We can succeed a lot more effectively if we do that. Don't be afraid to take a risk, but don't make the same mistake a second time." (Mr. R. – Financial Services)

651. "Don't give up. The best successes come from failures, but only if you are able to look back and analyze why you failed. I've made mistakes; I've done deals I shouldn't have done. Looking back, I wouldn't do them again. I couldn't see the forest through the

trees; almost every one of those bad deals was against my better judgment. I was second guessing myself." (Mr. D. – Real Estate)

NETWORKING

The most valuable members of your network are those who are least like you. Those who are most like you have little to offer in terms of fresh ideas and otherwise inaccessible avenues. But the real key is to make your networking mutualistic – to add value for others at least as much as you expect them to benefit you.

69.   "One must build relationships with people inside and outside of the industry. Form meaningful, genuine relationships with those within your company, but also with customers, competitors, civic and community leaders, and government leaders as well. This ensures the company has many connections with which to further its interests, and it provides additional avenues to pursue to take advantage of opportunities or confront threats." (Mr. D. – Financial Services)

76.   "Meet and befriend as many people as possible, and learn everything you can about them and from them. Always inquire about those you come in contact with because they will see that you care, and in return they will give you information or advice that could help you one day. They won't all be good contacts, but you will find those who are. Surround yourself with them because they are priceless. I have always made my greatest successes in business through a friend or someone I encountered along the way. People are the difference, no matter what level they are in the organization, so always respect those who are above you, around you, and beneath you." (Mr. L. – Hospitality)

111. "First and foremost, understand people. Business boils down to interactions between people or companies. Knowing all of the formulas and theories in the world may not help you deal with people effectively. You should build relationships and friendships with people not solely for a onetime benefit, but for a lasting relationship. This goes for customers, employees, suppliers, competitors, etc. How you cultivate relationships and deal with people will ultimately lead to your success or failure. I know numerous successful business managers and owners who have little or no formal education, but because they are personable and relate well to people, they are successful." (Mr. B. – Real Estate)

188. "Networking is an important factor for young professionals to move up in the right direction. Knowing the right people is half the battle. You have to be known to be wanted, so it is a great idea to pick the brains of those smarter than you. You always have something to learn. However, the most important thing I learned in business school is that nobody is smarter or better than you are, so given the right opportunities you really can achieve anything you want to." (Mr. G. – Conglomerate)

249. "Work on your relationships. This involves relationships within your team, organization, peer group, social network, family, and friends. Without these relationships you have nothing. Nobody can be successful without a support network." (Mr. F. – Healthcare)

324. "As far as getting into the professional world and improving your chances, you need to fully

understand just how important networking is. It took me a long time to understand the true value of contacts. You need to take advantage of meeting as many people as possible within your industry. Whether it's peers on lower levels or executives higher up, you can never be scared to expand your horizons. You need to take advantage of every possible opportunity that you can, whether it's within your industry or not." (Mr. S. – Financial Services)

341. "When you are in a job, network. Network with other people in the same industry somewhere else. Getting a network of people you can communicate with in your field is very important." (Mr. D. – Retailing)

351. "Whenever you come across an individual with whom you might work – a social, personal or business relationship – you have to ask three questions: 'Can I trust them? Do they care? Are they committed?' If you can answer yes to all three of those questions, you've got somebody you can go into battle with. You tend to find that those who can answer those three questions in your firm – those who do what is right, who do the best they can, and who treat other people with respect – they are your best. There's no magic to this; it's real straight forward." (Mr. W. – Energy, Mining & Materials)

355. "Have a good understanding of who you are so that you can develop relationships for networking." (Mr. K. – Energy, Mining & Materials)

391. "It's all about networking, connecting. Few really good ideas come when you are sitting at your

213

desk. Good ideas come from networking, partnering, communicating with others. Rarely can a CEO sit at his desk and develop great strategy; it first comes by talking to stakeholders and customers. You need lots of business cards, and you need to be out there a lot. It's not going to happen when you are in your office answering emails. You have to get out there." (Dr. K. – Healthcare)

397.   "Contacts are the way to move up anywhere. You should always keep 25 contacts on hand for any situation. I keep an Excel spreadsheet of 25 contacts that I know personally. Each one of them is so diverse in their industry, so if I ever need anything, I know who to call." (Mr. G. – Financial Services)

441.   "Network with every successful individual you encounter." (Mr. B. – Energy, Mining & Materials)

495.   "Always remember to treat everyone you meet with the utmost respect and professionalism. I am telling you this from personal experience. First impressions are extremely important; you never know who can help you in the future. One bad impression can take away an opportunity that you could never believe was possible. I am emphasizing the importance of properly networking. Anyone can meet an individual and place them in their networking circle, but this does not mean they are utilizing that contact to their full potential. It goes back to treating people with the utmost respect; if you do that correctly, then that individual will be more inclined to help you when you need it. You need to form and maintain a strong internal and external circle of contacts. Internally, you need to keep up with the direction you firm is going,

and make yourself available at all times. Do not hide in the distance, but make yourself visible to everyone in the organization. A good way to increase your network externally is by joining professional associations within your field of work. Network by attending as many meetings as possible, and always introduce yourself to unfamiliar people and establish a working relationship with them. Always remember to exchange contact information or business cards, and remembering to follow up is essential. I find it useful to maintain a database of contacts with as much information as possible, including phone numbers, e-mail addresses, as well as when and where you met that individual. Also, if you create a side note to help jar your memory and theirs, that seems to help spark conversation when you get in contact with them in the future. It is all about relationships, building them properly and keeping them strong. I am sure you have heard this phrase before, 'It is all about who you know and how you can leverage their expertise to your advantage.'" (Mr. S. – Information Technology)

500. "Thrive on making connections; you never know what may play out. One example: when my son was a sophomore in high school he met, per chance, a South Korean businessman at a soccer game. He was there on business. My son maintained a relationship through emails, and two years later he was invited to visit South Korea, stay with the family and travel. The visit turned into a strong relationship which led to a summer-long internship in China." (Mr. H. – Entertainment & Media)

505. "The most successful strategy is networking; you can't know too many people. It seems like

companies have so many choices, so they are hiring based on people that have networked with them. Networking can help get your foot in the door and get people interested in you for a job position. Interning is valuable; it's a type of networking that allows you to gain experience in the field." (Ms. L. – Consumer Products)

509. "There is no better time than now to develop a circle of contacts. This is a tool that will help you for many years. It's not easy to build it sometimes, but relationships are key – both within and outside of a company." (Mr. D. – Manufacturing)

551. "Make as many contacts as you can – I mean genuine contacts – so that people begin to see and know who you are and can see what kind of skills you have. That will come back to you as you begin to grow in your career." (Mr. R. – Financial Services)

PASSION

Be very alert to keep your passion other-focused. Getting that wrong by assuming that "Follow your passion" means to prioritize your own interests is a recipe for very limited perspective. If your passion is self-directed, your world will become very small. Our greatest successes, our most noble moments, our richest humanity come as we sacrifice self for the benefit of others. Think of those who have done that for you – parents, grandparents, patriots, leaders, mentors who have lived the principle that the purpose of life (and business) is to add distinctive value to the lives of others. There is powerful passion!

5.   "Passion is very deep. It takes many people a very long time to find out exactly what their passion is." (Mr. V. – Retailing)

6.   "It is always important to believe in your cause, so that you have more than just money to motivate you. You will then be successful."   (Mr. B. – Construction)

66.   "You must be extremely passionate in what you do. This is hard to come by and something you can't just fake. So be sure to find a company that believes in a lot of the same things you do." (Mr. F. – Financial Services)

116.   "I encourage students to always chase your passion, because you cannot succeed in strategic

management without a love for the people and the business. I confess that the demanding life of a CEO has taken away some of my passion for banking which always makes me second guess my past decisions." (Mr. Z. – Financial Services)

125. "Passion ultimately can lead to success, but often people can be blinded by their passion and are willing to cut corners and break rules to get to a desired outcome. My advice is to constantly follow your passion, but also keep your emotions in check and never make a decision without doing all the research and checking with your peers." (Mr. H. – Energy, Mining & Materials)

221. "Figure out where your passion lies. It is impossible to be a successful strategic manager if your career is merely a job. You have to love what you are doing, have a passion for success, and most importantly, believe that your success will make a difference in others' lives." (Mr. S. – Retailing)

224. "Have a sense of what kind of career you want. Find an organization that fits, and that you are passionate about. The passion needs to be driven by your co-workers, your customers, and the environment of the company so that your performance exceeds what is expected of you. Then, you will continue to progress and be rewarded. If you don't have fun at your job then it is all work. Once your job becomes all work then you lose motivation to exceed what is required of you and progress." (Mr. B. – Industrial Equipment)

231.   "Ask yourself, 'What do I love to do?' Find what you love and do that. And once you are doing what you love, practice, practice, practice. Learn and understand the fundamentals. Get to be an expert in that field. You will be much happier of a person if you are doing something that you love on a day-to-day basis for the rest of your life." (Mr. H. – Consumer Products)

269.   "Do what you are passionate about. If you are not passionate about something and if you do not enjoy it, get out of it. If you are passionate about something, you are going to be happier, you are going to have more energy, you are going to have conviction, etc. Whether you are leading an organization or aspiring to one day lead an organization, make sure you love what you do." (Mr. S. – Manufacturing)

274.   "The world is very different now than when I was beginning my career. But there are some rules that you can incorporate in your life that I believe can be everlasting. You must find something in your work that energizes you. Never settle for something you are not happy with or you cannot get excited about every day. It is also very important to work harder than the person to the right and left of you in order to have the most success in whatever field you choose to enter." (Mr. K. – Entertainment & Media)

279.   "I have walked away from jobs, and people would say, 'What the hell are you doing?' because I wasn't happy, and I wasn't doing what I wanted to do, and it didn't make me feel good. Sometimes I made mistakes, but most of the time I didn't. But I never had any money, so I had to obviously suck it up and work

some places where I really wasn't happy until I found something else. But the key is, end of the day, I see folks sitting around unhappy with their jobs for 10 years; that to me is paralyzing. You might as well go to work for the government; you might fit in very well there. But my advice to you will be to do what makes you feel good. Do what makes you feel happy, not what other people think of you, but what makes you feel good. You know what makes you feel good and what turns your knobs, so to speak, when you get up in the morning. You really feel good about whatever. And as you get larger in your career, you will find that you will get less opportunity to do that, but you still got to do some of it. I spend lots of time doing things I don't like to do, and there is no perfect job, but I always try to find opportunities for myself that really make me feel good about what I am doing. And what I am doing here is what makes me feel good. We are bringing in technology to a really antiquated industry. So that's what I like to do. And that's what I have done my whole career. When a window of opportunity ceases to exist, then I go, 'Bye-bye!' This may be the last place I stay. So just do what you like to do. It doesn't really matter whether other people like what you are doing or not. You will be much better in the long run. Don't get yourself stuck in some job that doesn't fulfill you. Yet sometimes it's not easy because we all have to make a living." (Mr. W. – Healthcare)

312.   "Go and find out what you love as it relates to your work. It might take a little while. You might not know what you truly love, or it might change. And when you know what you love, be yourself. I mean just be yourself, and hopefully the world will appreciate it. If being yourself is 'I want to be a

continuous learner,' then be a continuous learner. You know, life isn't all about these corporations. Life is about being a human being. You spend an enormous amount of time at work, so you want to be happy. So do what you love, and be yourself. I think the world ultimately rewards happier people who are doing what they really want to do, and they are authentically good at it. It's very different than just chasing something, you know. It takes a while to figure that out though. I don't pretend to think that's easy; everybody has to figure that on their own. That would be the bit of advice I would give." (Mr. V. – Consumer Products)

320. "Find something you get excited about. You have to find something that makes a 14 hour day seem short. If you cannot get excited about what you do, an eight hour day can seem very long. Look at me for example. We produce really boring products, but I get excited about my job because it has more to it than just the products. I am just thrilled to be in a position to travel, one that has all the international aspects to it. That's what gets me excited. If you are excited, you are willing to give 120%, and that's what you should do. Always give 120%. If you cannot find that in your first job, or maybe even in your second job, you will find it along the way. Just stay positive and keep a healthy attitude. That's important." (Mr. G. – Manufacturing)

334. "It is critically important that those starting new careers develop passion for the organizations they join and the jobs that they perform. Passion is really critical to be able to achieve success in anything. As difficult as it may be to land a desirable job, it is really important that the applicant really wants that opportunity, and

sees potential to develop passion in that role." (Mr. S. – Information Technology)

335. "Don't get a job for the sake of getting a paycheck. Try your best to figure out what you really love to do and pursue that. It's a cliché, but find what you love to do and go do that. I don't mean your first, second, or third shot at it will be the right one. If your first try doesn't get you there, don't be bashful about it. Keep looking. Keep looking until you find it. (Mr. D. – Business Services)

350. "Develop your passion. If you don't have a passion – if it is just a job – it is probably not the right job. You've got to enjoy it. You spend too much time at it. As we say around here, we spend more time at work than we do with our families. You've got to enjoy it. You have to develop a passion for, 'I want to do this.' There are a lot of people who will just get in jobs and stay in jobs, and it's just showing up everyday and going through motions. But I think you have to find a place where you can get excited and say, 'I could change this and make a difference.' Never before had I had any passion; I was not a big leader in school. But I got somewhere where I could make a difference. I mean, you've got to have some luck in life too. But really, it is passion." (Mr. H. – Financial Services)

376. "In knowing yourself, do you really have what it takes to be the CEO or President? Do you really have the 'want to'? A long time ago I had a saying I would say to myself that 'I can do whatever I want to do so long as I want to do it bad enough.' I went through some phases where I wasn't quite sure of that. But today I would say that you can do whatever you want

to do so long as you want it bad enough. And I really don't think that it's about whether you are some special person with all of these special gifts; if that was the case, I would have given up long ago. But I just mean when I say, 'Do you have what it takes?' I mean do you have enough grit? Do you have enough persistence about you to follow through? You must possess above-average determination." (Ms. T. – Transportation)

396. "Find something that you love to do, which you have the passion for and can work to the bone. Sooner or later you will win. The people that are rich and wealthy like doctors and lawyers are spending their time on the golf course; all you have to do is outwork them. That's what happens when people become successful; they get lazy, and they don't continue to do what they did to become successful. Sooner or later, somebody that has a passion for something will win. If you have passion for something and you work to your bone, you will win." (Mr. S. – Hospitality)

413. "Work. Just work. You can always learn from everything. Everything is a stepping stone. You learn from everything. If you hate it, you are still learning something – patience, determination, how to improve yourself. Know that everything is not going to be handed to you. Work is the most important thing. Work can be fun, but it does not have to be; you are not entitled to a fun job. But when you make the most of every situation that you're in, then you will eventually end up in the right situation. None of us are entitled to anything." (Ms. W. – Consumer Products)

422.   "Make sure you have a passion. If you don't, get out and find that path." (Mr. T. – Financial Services)

433.   "Find something you can be personally passionate about – not just advancing through the ranks. Then use your passion as fuel for a constant desire to learn." (Ms. T – Consumer Products)

450.   "You can tell someone is passionate when they can work 12-16 hours a day and they are still not tired. If you still have that energy and excitement, you never realize that you are tired." (Ms. B. – Food & Agriculture)

469.   "You know, great managers aren't in it for the money. I mean, the money is there; it has to be. But that isn't why they do it; it isn't what drives them. They're there because they love it. There is a thrill from getting the deal, accomplishing goals, or whatever. That is really what brings them back and makes them good. The money is there too – of course it is – but that isn't really what gets them going. It is really about opportunity." (Mr. C. – Business Services)

491.   "The advice that I would give you is that you will be the most successful manager when you find the field that you enjoy most. You have to like what you are doing to be a good manager, and I do not think you will be a good manager in a field that you hate. So it's vitally important to look deep inside yourself and search for what you truly enjoy and what you could see yourself doing for the next 30 years. That's the biggest piece of advice that I can offer. For your generation, finding that passion for something is much more difficult because there is so much pressure on just

finding a job in general that no one is taking the time to seek their dream." (Mr. S. – Construction)

494. "If you go to work in the morning and you don't like your job, then you need to find a different job. I wouldn't recommend just because you have an accounting degree that you make your lifelong challenge working in an accounting firm or an accounting department. After you give it an honest try and effort, and you aren't happy with what you're doing, then you need to find another line of work." (Mr. G. – Construction)

496. "Motivation and passion are huge. But you won't find a passion until you do something." (Mr. B. – Healthcare)

509. "You need to learn what you like and don't like. You may think you know, but till you get there you don't know because you are coming out of a different career – college – which is completely different." (Mr. D. – Manufacturing)

514. "Learn as much as you can about yourself. What really ticks you off? What are your passions and strengths? Take the time to know what you want to do for yourself. If you're not sure what your passions are, which is true for many young people, take baby steps in learning about yourself. Get involved in many activities and find what intrigues you the most." (Mr. O. – Energy, Mining & Materials)

518. "Don't get involved in something you don't honestly care about because you're not going to do well at it, and you're going to be perceived wrongly.

You're going to be perceived as lazy, unmotivated, unable to get along with others, obstinate." (Ms. K. – Consumer Services)

531.   "The thing that breaks my heart is young people that can't find what they want to do. Try selling insurance. Try selling Bibles door-to-door. Try driving a truck. Just find something and say, 'Man I dig this.' Find what you love to do, and then work the hell out of it." (Mr. S. – Hospitality)

PATIENCE AND PERSISTENCE

Do you see a paradox here? Seemingly contradictory values? Does persistence mean to press on regardless of any impediments or obstacles? Does patience imply indifference? Try this – the Tao Te Ching teaches that although water is soft and yielding, in time it penetrates even the smallest openings, and wears through the hardest resistance. This is the Yin of patience with the Yang of persistence. Adopt a long, broad view. When stuck, shift course never yielding – patient persistent perseverance.

78.   "Understand the virtue of patience. You have to realize when you are managing a company it is similar to putting together a puzzle. In order to put the different pieces together, you have to take a step back and analyze the different pieces and design a plan of action to see how they fit as a whole. Because companies possess different functions and encompass diverse people, CEOs have to understand how to treat each situation differently, so patience is required to be effective. Patience is a virtue that is necessary not only in business, but in life as well." (Mr. A. – Financial Services)

154.   "Nothing of value comes without hard work, passion and most importantly the ability to persevere. The difference between history's boldest accomplishments, and its most staggering failures is often, simply, the diligent will to persevere." (Mr. H. – Conglomerate)

243. "Persistence is the number one thing you must have to be successful. Very few people have started off with an idea, and become rich and by Year Five were a millionaire. So you have to be persistent and never give up. If you have to get a job at Burger King or washing cars, don't think of it as a lousy job you're doing just to make ends meet. Think of it as an opportunity to develop an idea or a relationship that eventually could be beneficial to you down the road." (Mr. W. – Business Services)

244. "It's a different generation. You must learn to be patient because everything has been so instantaneous for you; it wasn't like that 30 years ago. So find your weakest link and improve upon it; attack it until it's gone. Be determined." (Ms. C. – Manufacturing)

265. "An important trait is perseverance. There have been times I wanted to just quit, just chuck it and move on only to find that the goal was right around the corner. If we had quit, we wouldn't have reached the goal. Perseverance is key because you are always going to hit situations that discourage you. You're going to have naysayers. You're going to have things that get in your way, roadblocks that you didn't anticipate. But if you know it's the right thing to do, if you truly believe it's the right direction, and you truly believe in the goal, then perseverance is the key to getting there. That's true in anything in life – whether it was me trying to graduate from college, to me running an operation, to making it profitable – whatever it is, perseverance is the key to success." (Mr. G. – Healthcare)

278. "Use the right approach and remain persistent even when immediate results are not visible. Success will then surely follow you." (Mr. P. – Manufacturing)

292. "Persevering through the hard times is what taught me the most about being a CEO." (Mr. S. – Business Services)

301. "The most important thing to have in business is patience. The toughest thing I ever had to learn in my business experience is patience. When I was your age and someone didn't agree with me or they cut me short, it could be a pretty snappy fast conversation – didn't last long. In particularly in business if you can't have patience, you can't succeed. If you want to get a deal done so badly, you can taste it. If you push too hard in a deal, you will lose. In a deal, when you are out there trying to get an acquisition and you are over-anxious, they will see it. You can only push the deal at the pace it will go. Be patient. The other thing is never give up. You just have to persevere. There will be times you'll think, 'What did I get myself into?' But if you want to get to your ultimate goal and the end of the road, you have to persevere. You'll be knocked down. You will be told 'No' many times. Looking back on it, when I was trying to raise money for this project we were already in a tailspin. Nobody really knew it yet in early 2007. And it became apparent in 2008. When you hear 'No, No,' get back up and get on a plane over and over. If you pitch it long enough, you will eventually get what you are looking for. Some people could've been successful but couldn't persevere. It can get tough. It's not easy. But if you learn to be patient and persevere, you will be successful." (Mr. G. – Energy, Mining & Materials)

305.   "If you treat people fairly and do the right thing, you will get noticed. You're going to advance, but you've got to be patient. It doesn't come overnight; it comes with hard work and doing the right thing. So be patient; that's the other thing I tell people here. If you work hard, if you do the right thing, if you treat people fairly, good things are going to happen, and it gets recognized and rewarded. Might not be in the first year; you may have to work that teller job till something opens up. But if you are the best teller there is, something good's going to happen." (Mr. B. – Financial Services)

349.   "So many young people – I know because we interview them – want to be me. Well, I didn't get to be me – I'm 50 years old – by snapping my fingers. You have to earn those stripes. And that creates patience, diligence, perseverance. One thing for sure is the importance of having the tenacity to stick with something and see it through. Some people think, 'If I don't like this I will go another direction.' To continue to succeed you have to be committed to something through thick and thin, and keep your mind to it and stick to it. I think so many young people today will run instead of seeing it through. Don't ever accept no. Don't ever be willing to give up. I tell our young people this all the time. If you think you are being blocked by someone, our system is such that it allows you to find someone who will listen, so don't ever give up." (Mr. J. – Hospitality)

369.   "You have to be able to take risk, first of all. It is a long haul. It's not easy. You have to have a plan. You can't get anything overnight. You have to be

patient and you have to be willing to sacrifice." (Mr. K. – Consumer Products)

370.   "Don't go into a situation with guns blazing. Take some time to look around and see how it all functions before you start changing things." (Ms. I. – Food & Agriculture)

408.   "Understand that not every day is exciting. Not every day are you going to be challenged in your career. But that's just the way it is. For every exciting day there are many unexciting days, but that's all part of it. It takes much time and much effort to bring a result to fruition, and I think a lot of people that I run into, number one they don't have the work ethic. They just have no grasp of what a 40-hour a week job is, much less a 60- or 70-hour week that it really takes to be successful. The other thing that they have to grasp is that there's an element of mundane to what you do. There are just going to be some days where you have to equip yourself for the other days. You have to go through some mundane tasks to get to where you want. And I think it's very hard for a lot of people that expect every day to be exciting. So I think if you've got the work ethic – if you're willing to tolerate some degree of mundane – you will distinguish yourself through persistence. I think many people do not have persistence; that is very, very rare." (Mr. T. – Financial Services)

416.   "The key to being successful in this day and age is to be patient. We as Americans in today's culture often demand instant gratification and want a quarterly, monthly, weekly, and sometimes even a daily review of performance. A long-term mentality

may put someone who is early in their career behind in the short-term, but it will lead to a dramatically more successful career long-term. Be all about the long-term." (Mr. B. – Business Services)

449. "For those early in their careers I think it is important to display a great amount of patience. It is important for young professionals to take the time to listen and to learn from those around you that have a significant amount of experience. You can learn what you need to do, and what maybe you should not do, from all of the people around you. I also think it is important to understand that there really aren't any 'short-cuts' to success. If you want to be successful, you need to understand that it is going to take a lot of hard work, and it will take time. As my father used to always tell me, nothing that is worth having comes easy, and everything that is of value is in scare supply and hard to get. Remember that your career is much more a marathon than a sprint, and that if you take your time and listen and learn along the way, you'll be much better positioned for long-term success." (Mr. M. – Consumer Services)

548. "What advice would I give? Patience. You know, people blossom at different times. It's hard to be patient. We've all grown to like instant gratification. I'm constantly reminding myself to be patient. If you hire somebody in our business, its going to be a year before they start making any money. Its hard! But I've gotta pay this guy for a year before he produces. Those are the things you think about. So, patience." (Mr. G. – Business Services)

550.   "Hard work and dedication are truly the keys to success. You must be willing to start at the bottom, but that implies that you are ambitious enough to strive for the top. This takes unwavering determination. But never stop trying; perseverance reveals much about one's character." (Mr. T. – Consumer Services)

556.   "Be persistent. If someone says, 'We don't do it that way,' then you say, 'Let's talk about why we don't do it that way.' When someone tells you it can't be done, tell them, 'Okay, fine, let's talk about it.'" (Mr. N. – Energy, Mining & Materials)

595.   "Timing is everything. You may prepare yourself for a particular job or a career in something, but if the opportunity isn't there, it isn't there. So, be patient." (Mr. M. – Utilities)

611.   "To be successful, show that you have an undying persistence to meet your highest goals and the company should be quite interested in you." (Mr. W. – Healthcare)

614.   "Don't be discouraged. Persistence is the most important asset that you can have. Adversity is your friend early in your career." (Mr. D. – Information Technology)

618.   "Don't be greedy. Don't argue or fight over money. Be patient; don't worry about conquering the world right now." (Mr. Z. – Financial Services)

621.   "I would urge a young professional to be patient in terms of what you're doing and the salary related to it. If you're getting a good experience that

doesn't necessarily have great pay, it will end up benefitting you in the long run. Often, people will pass up what's best for them chasing a few extra dollars." (Mr. F. – Manufacturing)

624.   "The company doesn't owe you anything. The company is giving you an opportunity. That's why I say be patient, and plan to persevere." (Mr. H. – Financial Services)

628.   "Be persistent, and don't be discouraged if things don't fall into place immediately. Be open-minded; things change." (Mr. W. – Financial Services)

PRIORITIES

When we together establish and fully commit to a system of values that clearly lays out what matters most, what matters quite a bit, what matters some, what matters a little, and what does not matter, then our priorities become a focused tool for making solid decisions in the midst of complexity. Imagine working for a person, or an organization, that doesn't have clear values or stable priorities. Be a beacon. Lead the way!

42.　"No matter what industry you are in, you must be centered on the values and mission of the organization. Figure out what is important to you. Figure out what matters most to you." (Mr. W. – Consumer Services)

149.　"MBAs need to know what they really want out of a business and who the beneficiaries would be. It's not just about profitability. Talk one-on-one with the investors, but also all your stakeholders. Figure out exactly what they are looking for. On top of it all, working for the common good should be your first priority." (Mr. G. – Information Technology)

159.　"You have to inventory your assets. You must rank and prioritize your time and talents to get the most out of every day. This separates highly effective people from the mediocre ones." (Mr. J. – Conglomerate)

373. "As a manager, your priorities change as you get older. When you're younger you focus more on the facts whereas older managers tend to focus on the people." (Mr. M. – Financial Services)

418. "If you are really serious about accomplishing something in the business world, you have to start out with the idea that it is going to come first and foremost in your life. Do the extra things in the beginning. On your first job, get there early and stay late. Do what you need to do and a bit extra. Seek to increase your responsibility at ever chance you get. Try to be more valuable to the people around you. Don't be afraid to do the extra things." (Mr. F. – Business Services)

419. "If I could go back and give myself a word of advice in my freshman year of college, I would tell myself not to take my education so seriously – to relax and have fun, but really have a balanced educational experience." (Ms. B. – Consumer Services)

440. "It's hard to be in three different meetings in different states at the same time, so you really have to prioritize your main concerns and think about what needs attention first." (Mr. S. – Consumer Products)

445. "Also, give back to the community. It's not always about making money. Being involved in local charities and events is a great way to give back to your customers and employees." (Mr. R. – Financial Services)

461. "I really believe that one of the best things you can do – and this is what we do here because it gives us our foundation – is write down your goals and commit to those goals and set dates to accomplish

those goals. If anyone does that – truly commits to their goals – then they are bound to increase their success factor. Never be self-satisfied." (Mr. H. – Business Services)

490. "Don't measure success by money. I have always said that I measure success by the number of people's lives I've touched in a positive way – where I make a difference in their lives. So I measure my success not by the dollars, not by the houses and things like that, but the difference I make." (Mr. R. – Healthcare)

493. "The moral of that story is, try and know as much – that self-awareness piece – I mean really pick yourself apart and be candid about how you are put together and where your interests are. I wrote my obituary in 1988. The important thing is to walk to the end of your life and look back, and write down what it is you will have achieved or left behind. It's been a complete guiding force for me because it has helped me keep, in very clear focus, the three things the matter. Those three things, for me at least, are raising a successful family, running a successful business, and giving something back to the community. I think there's a certain amount of life planning, and then I think you've really got to come to grips with you are – your true strengths and weaknesses – and so build that high level of self-awareness. Then decide how to apply it; I don't think that there is a right or a wrong answer because it is your life to lead, no one else's. It comes back to self-awareness and learning from experience. If you think about it, no one's going to help you in life, really. Ultimately, you've got to be self-guiding; it's down to you. Your life will be what you make of it – and, I mean, your parents can give

you advice – but ultimately it is going to come down to what you decide to make of it. Somewhere out there you need to develop feedback mechanisms so you can stay on course. Somewhere you have to have a plan. Somewhere you have to have an end goal in mind. Somewhere it has to be laced with reality. Even if I wanted to be the King of England, it isn't going to happen. So somewhere out there there is a reality check that just keeps you grounded. You come across a lot of people that say, 'I want to be a CEO.' They have no clue what it means – no clue how to get there – it just sounds good." (Mr. B. – Consumer Products)

494. "After time you figure out what's most important in your life. It just depends what phase of your life you're in. You need to decide what your priorities are. Here it was family first, work second, and everything falls into line. There's a lot more to life than money, but money is a driver." (Mr. G. – Construction)

595. "Know who you are and what your real priorities are. Don't worship the dollar so much that you become someone who you are not." (Mr. M. – Utilities)

664. "If your priorities are not in order, once you get to the top, nothing will be awaiting you." (Mr. W. – Manufacturing)

669. "Make everything you do revolve around your core values. Others will look to you as a leader, so if you waver on anything you say or how you live, you will lose their respect." (Mr. S. – Financial Services)

PROBLEM SOLVING

It is clear that life and business are integrated. The principles of success and satisfaction in each are the same: Focus on the needs and wants of others; help them with their issues; offer them a better way. Extrinsic rewards and intrinsic satisfaction will flow to you naturally.

21.   "Look at problems as processes. Let your staff and employees know that you are troubleshooting the process, not the people. If you approach things from this perspective, people will cooperate and open up regarding issues you need to hear about." (Mr. I. – Business Services)

91.   "It's important to learn how to assess situations and apply the tools you have learned and your own experiences to the situation at hand. MBAs must be able to precisely define where opportunities are and assess the situation correctly." (Mr. T. – Hospitality)

113.   "Stop, take a step back, and think logically about the situation at hand. I see the ambition possessed by MBAs, and I see this as a great positive, but it can also be one of your largest weaknesses because you may be in too big of a rush to solve the problem. You must first fully understand the problem. The second point MBAs must understand is that every answer does not reside in the computer. I see too many people try come up with a solution from a computer program, but they have not thought the problem through fully. Often times they cannot fully explain the solution they arrived at, which is a sign that they truly

do not understand the problem in the first place. Lastly, I would like to stress the importance of thinking logically. I believe that you will succeed in the business world if you can logically think through puzzles and problems." (Dr. H. – Financial Services)

210.   "For career success in today's business world, the two most important qualities a person should have are learning and problem-solving. In this age of information and technology overload, the ability to quickly sort through information, discern what is in it, and learn it faster and better than the other person gives you an advantage. Problem-solving is then effectively applying this information. Most people think that knowledge is power, but knowledge is worthless unless we use it. Remember, the essence of real-world problem-solving is to fill in the blanks. It is easy to pick an option when you are already presented with a set of options. But the person who is really valuable is the one who can think of the options. Think of a customer asking the question, 'How do we improve our delivery performance?' We would have to be able to take this broad question and understand its various components. We have to start by understanding what this term means, what steps it involves, who executes it, how it is measured. Once we have the facts, figuring out the rest is a personal, individual brainstorming exercise to come up with options. If we can successfully go through these steps and come up with a good set of options, then we create tremendous value for our customers. This is why I feel that learning and problem solving are the two most valuable skills you need to have in business today. Exercising these every day, and evaluating yourself against these standards, is very important for success in

today's business world." (Mr. S. – Information Technology)

220. "I think that the education you're receiving provides you with a foundation of how to think. If you get a good education, it's not the facts you are memorizing or the answers to the questions that I am giving you, it's the way you apply logic and the way you think about circumstances. So when you go out into the world and when you start to work, whether it's for the head of a business, or you're pursuing a passion, or working in a barn, the real value comes into that organization when you put yourself in that organization's shoes. When you're thinking 'How will we do this better?' 'How can we improve these opportunities?' and when you take it personally. When you apply the foundation that you know, when you continue to learn from what you're doing, and when that is something an employer loves." (Mr. Z. – Business Services)

282. "I would say my advice would be to get into places where the action is, and that's usually, though not always, in the pain points of an organization. These are the places where there are opportunities to improve upon, or where the company is struggling with challenges. If I were starting out today, I would look for an opportunity where I could definitely make a difference to either the company's top line or bottom line in the near term. You know, like in three months, six month, nine months, or something like that. Just out of school, you've got a lot of skills and a lot of tools that frankly the people in the companies you go work at don't have. They're either new or never learned. You have a lot to offer. I think the question

always has to be if you want to be successful in any endeavor, what can you do for the company, not what the company can do for you to paraphrase the great President." (Dr. S. – Manufacturing)

307.   "Do everything you can do to always look at yourself instead of others, and ask, 'What can I do to improve the situation?'" (Mr. G. – Manufacturing)

512.   "I look for managers that are willing to take on calculated risks. I tell my managers, 'Don't bring me problems; bring me solutions.' Remember, you must recruit employees who are willing to work hard at what they do." (Mr. E. – Manufacturing)

548.   "Someone said to me once, 'What makes a great agent?' and I think they were waiting for the answer 'Oh, the one who brings in the most money.' That's not it, not with me. It's the guy who solves the problems the fastest. How good are you at solving problems? That's what we're dealing with here. We're dealing with people and money, and those two things create problems. I don't care how you cut the cake, every day I'm dealing with problems because of those two things. Now, that's a good thing because that's how we make money, but it creates problems. Now, you gotta figure out how to solve them, and you gotta figure out how to solve them quickly. And the guy that solves them the quickest, he's a winner. Give me a problem in the business and I'll figure out the solution in seconds because that's how I was taught. That's how I was mentored; those are the people I've worked for. I worked for a guy, no matter what problem you gave him, he hit it out of the park in two seconds." (Mr. G. – Business Services)

589. "An MBA doesn't make you brilliant. It makes you a fine-tuned, organized thinker and problem-solver. Come ready to use those tools to help enhance what you do. Use those skills to meet customer needs." (Mr. V. – Healthcare)

593. "Organizations promote people who are problem solvers. So welcome any opportunity to solve new challenges. If you are successful in that, and work for a decent company, the rewards and promotions will take care of themselves." (Mr. G. – Information Technology)

RISK

We run the risk of misunderstanding risk. Too often we say, "Big risk, big returns." Not so fast. Try this instead, "Big risk, big imagined returns." We hope. Now reverse the implied causation: if we want outsized returns, we are sure to be exposed to outsized risks. That relationship is for sure, nothing imagined there. It is a fine distinction, but critical. And risk is vital – necessary for life. So when you feel like shying away, remember this old saying, "Great ships are always safe if they stay in the harbor. But that is not why we build great ships." You are that ship; it's why others have invested so much in you. Go forth!

46.   "The difference between a man of knowledge and a wise man is the willingness to take and measure risks. A wise man has taken risk and both succeeded and failed. A man of knowledge simply watches what is going on around him but is unwilling to take risks. You hope that you have more success than failure, but by taking risks you are almost guaranteed to fail at times. You cannot let those failures make you timid from trying new things and taking the risks. Strategic management is about taking risks, but also developing the ability to evaluate risk. I see a lot of people make decisions to do something that fails because they were not able to accumulate the facts and evaluate the facts necessary to adequately measure the risks associated with the decision to proceed with something. Had they been good at that they would never have proceeded

with the effort because they would have determined that it was too risky and very likely to fail. Too many people just roll the dice and hope for success. They don't do their homework to identify and measure the risks of their proposed effort." (Mr. M. – Entertainment & Media)

85. "First and foremost, you need to be able to evaluate risks. If you do not have the ability to do this, you will not excel. You have to have the propensity to take risks, and to get outside of your comfort zone. Most people look at the downside when they really need to be focusing on the upside, or the positive aspects of business. It is imperative to be positive in order to make things work within the organization." (Mr. T. – Manufacturing)

147. "Strategic management requires taking risks, and students should not be afraid of doing that. Frequently, for job security reasons, students refuse to take on some risks and miss opportunities for advancement, learning, and exploration. So I advise students to constantly take on new challenges and keep in mind the fact that will likely not stay in one spot forever." (Mr. B. – Healthcare)

245. "Take on more than you think you can handle, even if that means you have to work for free. Ask to be challenged; it's okay to fail." (Mr. S. – Food & Agriculture)

271. "Be willing to take risks. The only certainty is uncertainty. Stay curious. Be okay with failure. You have to be a gambler – not a Las Vegas gambler, but gamble with what you know. It's okay to have a

contrary view, so long as you support it. Stay fluid."
(Mr. G. – Retailing)

304.   "Don't be afraid to take risks, especially when
you are young. There are a lot of C students running
companies in this world because they were willing to
take risks. And there are a lot of smart people out there
who could have made a lot more of a splash in the
world but were scared to take the risk. Just because
you fail once, don't be scared to take the risk again and
keep trying." (Mr. S. – Construction)

359.   "I don't see how you can ultimately be
successful in business if you don't take risks. Business is
almost like any competitive game. It's requires killer
instinct because you are never assured of winning. You
have to decide where you're going to apply your
resources and where you're going to battle. You can't
be all things to all people. You also can't just sit back
and wait for things to happen in global business today.
We are challenged in every country. If you sit back and
wait for something to happen, those guys will eat you
alive." (Mr. J. – Healthcare)

378.   "I feel that young people cannot be scared to
take a risk or make a mistake. You've got to get out
there and commit yourself fully and wholeheartedly to
a path, and not look back to think 'Was this right or
wrong decision?' Only by totally immersing yourself
and surrounding yourself with your work and your
customers will you be able to fully achieve what you
are capable of." (Mr. S. – Real Estate)

399.   "Think about the kind of life you want to have
when you are in your career. I have seen many, many

people get burned out from working 70 hours a week for years and years. Realize that other things are important too. Plus, when you are working all those hours when you start your career, you are underpaid! I think that it is important for a person in your position to understand the power of being unique. This is the time in your life to take risks. You could even start your own business, even though it could likely fail. If you can get access to capital, it would be a good time to take huge risks now before you get in the hole of having to provide for endless payments and also a family. It's much easier on you to fail when you're young than when you are older and more established in your career. Right now, it would be a unique learning experience for you. For someone like me, it would be a complete disaster. Take a chance and do something interesting and challenging because there is the chance you could be very successful. If not, it is something interesting and fun to talk about with people and will surely make you stand out. In hiring someone, I would much rather see that than someone trying to climb a corporate ladder." (Mr. F. – Manufacturing)

426. "When you achieve something – your family, financial success, anything important to you – defend it; do not take unnecessary risks with what you value. Just make what I call 'measured gambles.'" (Mr. C. – Energy, Mining & Materials)

500. "Learn to be comfortable in uncomfortable positions. If you are ever going to grow, you must be willing to take risk and deal with an ever changing environment which is uncomfortable for natural human behavior." (Mr. H. – Entertainment & Media)

508. "Take calculated risks and don't be afraid to make mistakes – everyone makes them – but use common sense. Be patient, but take good opportunities. Never get too comfortable with where you are." (Mr. H. – Food & Agriculture)

520. "Don't be afraid to take chances! At every turn you will be faced with decisions that are tough, but do not be afraid to make one. The worst-case scenario is you freeze and make no decision. Who cares if you screw up? God knows I have screwed up plenty of times, but out of each of those comes a new appreciation for success." (Mr. B. – Manufacturing)

525. "Be aggressive; don't be afraid of taking risks. Make your own luck." (Mr. W. – Transportation)

551. "Be flexible – that is to say, don't be afraid to try anything. But question everything. Don't throw caution to the wind, but if someone says, 'I have an idea for something that I would like for you to try to do,' – a new job – hear them out. Think about it. What is the opportunity? Is it something worth trying? Manage your risks so you don't bet the whole farm, but be willing to take some measured risks." (Mr. R. – Financial Services)

640. "You are young without a lot of the overhead – kids and family – so you're at a point now where I took a lot of my risks. I took a lot of my risks early when I had no kids so I didn't feel negligent as a father." (Mr. S. – Healthcare)

649. "Students should work on their risk tolerance skills. They should be able to take career risks, be able

to take on assignments other people do not want to do. You should use risk as a personal asset to your advantage." (Mr. B. – Entertainment & Media)

STRATEGIC PLANNING

Everything we do – in business or in life – can benefit from thinking and acting strategically: blending the art of intuition with the science of analysis, being holistic and long-term oriented, all to the end of creating distinctive value for others.

20.   "Learn how to think and evaluate the true causes of a business situation. In order to set correct policy, a strategic manager must know what causes have led the company to its current situation. Once he knows this, he can then adjust the strategy accordingly. However, this is no easy task. It involves sifting through all the information available and being able to identify which information is applicable to that decision. That is the challenge." (Mr. N. – Consumer Products)

36.   "In order to be an effective strategist you must not only understand your company, its products or services, the environment in which you operate, and the customers you serve, but also to know your competition. The best way to do so would be to stay in touch with your employees as much as possible, allowing them to provide input and information about what's going on and what direction the company should be going. Staying in touch and in good communication with your people and customers will guide you when planning the future direction of the company." (Mr. B. – Construction)

40.   "When making strategic decisions, your competitors in most cases are going to do the obvious. It is the job of the strategic thinking manager to think

logically, but to think in a different way. This is how companies gain competitive advantage. Do not get set in your ways. Just because a strategy worked in one situation does not mean that strategy will work in another. Every situation is different with its own unique set of circumstances. Take each situation for what it is and evaluate all the issues surrounding the situation. This does not mean that you cannot draw from past experience; just don't get caught up in one method." (Mr. B. – Manufacturing)

41.   "Always look to the future for paradigm shifts in the world's culture. And let your competitor go into battle first because the last troops in usually win the war." (Mr. M. – Information Technology)

43.   "The plan that you spend months on doesn't mean a thing unless you implement it. And you can't implement it without the buy-in of a lot of people. And you can't implement it without a lot of follow through on the execution of it. So learn to follow through. Great plans to do not fail because they are poor plans, they fail because of execution. That is the most difficult thing. It's critical." (Mr. D. – Healthcare)

54.   "Strategic management involves understanding the business that you are working in, but at the same time being able to look at that business for the future. It involves being able to ask how you are going to get better, and how you are going to move the organization forward. Not only do you have to have a vision, but you must also be able to identify the resources that are necessary to execute that vision. You can have the best plan in the world, but if you don't execute it doesn't matter. Don't get so wrapped up in

the vision or the plan that you disassociate it from the actual execution. I've seen companies that have these beautiful strategic visions for the future, but they can't translate those visions into business plans that actually support the vision, and thus they fail." (Ms. H. – Financial Services)

69. "To completely understand and, consequently master strategic management is a difficult, complex task. Realistically, this may be more of an unattainable goal – like chasing a rainbow. You can come close to the source of the image – the mist in the air and the sunlight that refracts to form the brilliant colors – but you can never actually reach the rainbow. Becoming an excellent strategic manager requires constant adaptation and change, for the environment in which any manager is operating in is not only fluid, it is often turbulent, sometimes violently so." (Mr. D. – Financial Services)

83. "Strategy so infiltrates the organization that it is difficult to separate it from the daily operations. It is very difficult to say what is strategy and what is not strategy because strategy is messy. I feel that a strategic manager should pause every few months and make sure it is clear what strategy the organization is trying to achieve." (Mr. D. – Retailing)

84. "Always have a backup plan because nothing ever goes as planned." (Mr. K. – Manufacturing)

94. "Strategic planning is a brain exercise that has no value whatsoever unless you know how to bring it to life. It has to be consumer-driven. We cannot just sit around and talk intellectually about strategic

management; we actually have to put it into action, and therefore bring it to life." (Mr. B. – Retailing)

96.   "Commitment, consistency, and adjustment are the three things that MBAs need to know about strategic management. A successful strategic manager must have a vision and never waver too far away from that vision. But at the same time, they have to allow for failure and make adjustments along the way. Consistency is important throughout the process so that managers don't get too excited when things are going well, or too depressed when things are going poorly. Successful managers are able to endure the cycles and sustain long-term profitability while satisfying other criteria too." (Mr. M. – Manufacturing)

97.   "Everything starts as a strategy. You strategically determine where you are going. And once you figure out strategies, you execute them." (Mr. H. – Energy, Mining & Materials)

102.   "Successful doers have to transition to strategic thinkers. Look for ways to apply strategic thinking to your current job, your future career plans, and your life. Remember that strategic thinking is multi-faceted; you have to understand lots of different parts. A strategic manager must be able to draw on many experiences, so look for opportunities to get exposure to different parts of business. Challenge the way you think about things. Think multiple steps ahead. What will or could the competitive reaction be? Always allow yourself time to think, and learn how you think best and in what situations. Creating effective strategy is learning what not to do. You can't go after all opportunities." (Mr. H. – Consumer Products)

103. "Many graduates come out of school with grand ideas, but are unable to implement the ideas. Most beginning jobs allow very little strategic planning, if any at all. That ability will come with time and experience. Meanwhile, a recent graduate needs to take time and make use of it to gain experience, realize opportunities, be active in decisions and discussions, and to build skills necessary to make strategic decisions. Strategic management is a craft. It takes experience and instruction to practice the craft well." (Mr. A. – Pharmaceuticals)

109. "You have to understand your vision and how that vision drives strategy. From there your strategy is based on what the options are. It's about building scenarios and coming to the few that are most likely. Then it is about how to evaluate those scenarios. You have to be able to model them. It really gets into what is the basis of the direction you want to go? From there it's how you measure it. If you can't measure a strategy or the results of a strategy, then you really can't adopt it. For me it's all about the measurements. It's about understanding the basis for choosing one strategy over another, and being able to measure that. Understand and execute!" (Mr. M. – Information Technology)

119. "Do you know how to play chess? Strategic management is very similar to a game of chess. To execute your strategy, your timing has to be right on. You have to have vision – long-term vision. Some are better at thinking strategically than others, especially in this day and age when everything is in the present, instant, now! The excellent strategic thinker is looking ahead, preparing long-term, planning three moves from now, just like in chess." (Mr. K. – Hospitality)

121.   "Strategic management applies to every facet of life, whether it is in business or your personal life. The first thing you must know is that you can base your initial reasoning on broad theoretical terms, but you must never stop there. Management by textbook case studies is just a disaster waiting to happen. Since all variables are controlled by and directly impact human beings, I stress the value of understanding people. When you make a decision that is going to alter the landscape of a company, you should take a step back and think about what this change will bring about for all of your stakeholders. Limiting the use of textbook theory and taking a personal touch helps limit negative personal impacts on all stakeholders." (Mr. G. – Healthcare)

128.   "You need to understand how to become close to your customers and employees, take into account their ideas, and apply them to your strategies In order to grow." (Mr. N. – Hospitality)

138.   "Strategic management requires taking yourself out of the day-to-day activities and getting a bigger vision of where you want to be and what your organization's about. You can't get stuck in the day-to-day activities. You have to get out of that. You can't think about it. You have to look over a horizon and make an assumption that the daily activities will be fine in order to decide where you want to take the organization. It's broad. It's a macro look as opposed to a micro look at an organization's cultural patterns. That requires you to get yourself on the outside looking in. This is why leaders take their management teams away from the company for a few days off-site to allow for free thinking." (Mr. F. – Manufacturing)

141.   "You need to think strategically before you even begin to act tactically. You cannot dive right into the problem; you have to sit back and analyze every aspect of the situation. You have to strategically align your long-term performance objectives with your course of action. The key is to understand that strategic management does exist, and it exists for a good reason." (Mr. H. – Energy, Mining & Materials)

142.   "It is irrelevant for college students to think about strategic management until they have 20 to 25 years of experience. The most important thing to do is to find a position that adds value to the organization. When that happens, advancement and reward are almost automatic; the stakes become larger and larger over time, and one's role in an organization will gradually become less analytic and more strategic." (Mr. D. – Transportation)

158.   "You've got to try to figure out the one or two real advantages that your company has and focus on those. This is how you build a company. What are the things that really set you apart? Figure out how that fits into the overall marketplace and where you want to go. Focus on the real differentiators that you have." (Dr. A. – Healthcare)

164.   "The devil is in the details. Once you have a strategic vision, the hardest thing to do is to implement it. You can have a great strategy, but if you don't do well with implementation, it doesn't make any difference how great your strategy is. You must take the time to dot the i's and cross the t's." (Mr. S. – Food & Agriculture)

168.   "If you let your natural skills take over, and you are in touch, aware, and have a good team behind you, then the strategy will come to you." (Mr. G. – Healthcare)

170.   "Extreme care needs to be used when contemplating diversification. The risks involved in branching off into a new product must be analyzed thoroughly to ensure you keep your competitive advantage, maintain profitability, and remain within your corporate vision." (Mr. K. – Information Technology)

211.   "Reality can be very different from what you may hear in the classroom, or see being discussed on TV, or in books on management. Typically, this is presented as a prescription, a list of things to do; as long as a CEO more or less follows it, then he or she will be successful. In reality, there are many variations of successful leaders. I know a lot of CEOs in our industry, and many of them are very effective. At the same time, I see a huge diversity in terms of how they approach the job, how they run their companies, and what they consider to be important in order to succeed. There is not just one formula for being successful. A lot of different kinds of approaches can work depending on a situation." (Dr. B. – Business Services)

217.   "Plans are a process. For an organization to be successful, you need to drive the planning process down through the organization. You need to get good ideas to come from the top, and elicit goal congruence – get everyone on the same page. Also, good strategic planning should be continuous, not something you do once and then put on the shelf. It's about

communicating up and down in the organization." (Mr. F. – Construction)

221. "Strategic management involves bringing together a variety of skill sets, some of which can be taught and others which are either innate or only learned with real-world experience. They include analytical ability, creativity, marketing acuity, vision, and leadership skills. Very few folks have all of the skills necessary to be successful strategic leaders." (Mr. S. – Retailing)

231. "One thing students need to understand about strategic management is you have to evaluate your plan. Ask yourself, 'Should we be in this business or not?' and 'Should we keep going or not?' If the answer is yes, then you have to completely understand how you plan to attack this business. Keep the plan easy to execute and make it common sense." (Mr. H. – Consumer Products)

235. "It is too easy to get caught up in tactical operations that people don't put enough focus on the strategic side of the equation. Most people in their careers start out tactically in operations and that's the focus they continue to put on things. They don't ever differentiate in their mind that there is a difference between strategic thinking and tactical thinking. So it is clear that winners are the people who appreciate that strategy does exist and is alive and well, and he who masters it will be the one who does well." (Dr. T. – Healthcare)

282. "A brilliant strategy without an execution plan is worthless, and flawless execution of a flawed

strategy is worse than worthless. I mean it's dangerous. So the stakes for having a good strategy are high. And you know, as we talked about how companies with good strategies win, and ones with poor strategies don't. So the stakes are high, and if all it is is a pile of paper in a drawer that you do because you've always done it or your board insists you do it, then you're just wasting your time. I personally think that strategic planning is one of the most fun parts of my job. And I love it when a plan comes together and it's messy, messy. It never happens the way you think it will happen. People don't like change. They don't like getting on board with the new strategy. But you know, it takes a lot of perseverance, but it's really one of the four primary jobs of the CEO so it's worth spending time on. And it's worth spending time on thinking about how you'll execute it." (Dr. S. – Manufacturing)

291.   "An MBA is directed at training you to think strategically, like a CEO, to think holistically, and at 360 degrees. Continue thinking at that level; bring in your own responsibilities and those of your company. This may be a hard task for a lot of young professionals, but this will gear you to think outside of your day-to-day tasks, your own goals within your job, and to think what these inputs are doing for your organization as a whole. Always be asking, 'How can it be improved?' or 'What can I do to help with other supporting or secondary actions that surround my job function?' Approach the issues you see day- to-day by learning how to write, organize, and communicate like a CEO of a company." (Mr. B. – Manufacturing)

320.   "I think it is important for students to understand the difference between strategic and

tactical. It's not the same but a lot of students think it is. The realization of strategy is something you learn with experience. I think that it is a necessity for students to learn about strategic management in school. In my opinion it is part of a basic education." (Mr. G. – Manufacturing)

322. "I think a lot of people get caught up in and enjoy planning for eight to ten years down the road. In my experience this is just a waste of time and resources. Three years out is about as good as you're going to hit it." (Mr. C. – Food & Agriculture)

327. "The advice I would give is to be very thorough. Think. Strategy is hard work. It is not necessarily just a stroke of brilliance that comes and it's all worked out. It's hard work figuring out details, making sure you understand the markets, making sure you understand opportunities, products, pricing, all those things that go into strategic management. So again, the advice I would give is just to be very thorough and hard working; cover the details." (Mr. H. – Hospitality)

335. "What I would call strategic management goes back to leadership versus management. Strategic management is all about leadership. Managers manage the day-to-day; strategic thinkers are always thinking about where we are headed. I can't imagine being younger and interested in business and not wanting to be a strategic manager. That's what the future is all about. It's where entities are headed rather than where they've been – sort of like being an astronaut instead of a history major. You should think about which personality type are you, and if you're the kind who

wants to be a leader and wants to develop new, better, different things, then strategic management should be an interesting route to go." (Mr. D. – Business Services)

341.   "Strategic planning needs to be something that you can validate. You can't make stuff up. You cannot base it on hope. You have to base it on valid reasoning. Some people hope things will occur: 'I hope we will get a 10% increase.' But show me on paper where it is coming from; reason it out and prove it to me. That's what you need to understand; you have got to prove anything that you put into a strategic plan. If it can't be proved, then you need to say that this is our hope. Then it really isn't a strategic plan; it is a hope plan." (Mr. D. – Retailing)

372.   "A CEO's responsibility is to maximize the overall performance of the firm. To achieve this objective, CEOs must analyze the drivers of the firm's current performance and identify external changes that may affect this performance. On this basis, their job is then to find ways to better leverage the firm's human capital and financial resources in order to sustainably improve performance. At the corporate level, a CEO's responsibility is also to define the scope of the firm's activities, to implement strategic moves that will affect this scope, and convince shareholders, employees, and customers of the relevance of their strategy. As a newly hired MBA, you will not only need to understand, share and implement the strategy of your company, you will also be required to participate in shaping it." (Mr. H. – Healthcare)

380.   "Believe your research. Do it and believe it, and create a core value system that you repeat to

yourself every day. For us, it's 'clean, safe, well lit, entertaining and good value.' We say it over and over and over again. I believe that the simpler you can keep it, the more successful you can be. This is pretty simple stuff, not rocket science. I'm not Ken Blanchard; I'm just an old country boy." (Mr. S. – Entertainment & Media)

382.   "Don't overlook the old basic things that are out there. There are still lots of opportunities to be had from activities that you might find in everyday life. There are lots of opportunities in low tech industries." (Mr. F. – Conglomerate)

384.   "Strategic management is two main things. The first thing is that the devil is in the details. The second thing is that it is 20% strategy and 80% execution. Strategy does not guarantee results; it is execution that guarantees results. Just having the theoretical knowledge that an MBA provides, and having the ability to put together a good theoretical strategy does not ensure that this strategy will deliver expected results. You need to make sure that the strategy is executable and that the execution is also planned out. Without the execution, the strategy is nothing. Strategic management is like charting a flight plan. But you also have to know how to fly the plane. Just having the flight plan does not mean that you are going to meet your goals. The devil truly is in the details. It is not enough to strategize at a 30,000 foot level. The plan has to include details even at the ground level. Then, of course, you have to ensure that these plan details are followed and executed." (Mr. H. – Manufacturing)

392.   "The strategic aspects of management require you to be fully aware of what is going on around you, as well as being lucky enough to be in the right places at the right or wrong times in order to succeed." (Mr. H. – Energy, Mining & Materials)

398.   "There is no successful CEO that hasn't enjoyed a huge amount of luck in being in the right place at the right time. There is a lot of work, but it has to do with luck." (Mr. R. – Consumer Products)

414.   "Think about how you think before you buy something, or how you want to be treated when you get work done on your car. With these small insights you build a strategic mind." (Mr. M. – Healthcare)

421.   "You need to understand that honesty, integrity and heart are the three big things driving strategic management. It doesn't matter how many books you read or how many nights you lie awake thinking, if you don't understand those three things, then you will come out on the losing end. There will come a time when you will be glad you have those three things in your corner." (Mr. R. – Financial Services)

447.   "You can have the best strategic plan in the world, but if you don't have the resources to do it, your plan is meaningless." (Mr. S. – Healthcare)

449.   "I think it is important to understand that establishing the strategy of a company should be based upon a significant amount of research and empirical data to support the strategies of the company. The strategy of a company is the direction that it will take going forward, and it must include the means by which

they will get to the ultimate destination. I don't believe that this process can occur effectively without a significant amount of data to support what it is you are setting out to do as an organization." (Mr. M. – Consumer Services)

450.   "A CEO has to have a strategy, and to enact the management of that strategy. If I didn't, then I would feel like a boat out in the ocean without a sail – just going to go wherever the current or tide takes me. When I have strategic goals, I have that sail and I sail toward those goals with as many people in my boat to run with me toward our goals." (Ms. B. – Food & Agriculture)

458.   "Strategic management requires a manager who is thoughtful, unperturbed, calm, and who is willing to look under every rock and discover every good and bad fact about his business. You have to be listening to people, talking to people, asking, testing. Really, the key step to being a good strategic manager is to be a sponge, always taking everything in. A good strategic manager has to have clear objectives that are measurable, definable, and which they watch on a regular basis along with everyone who works in the business. Then again, a sponge, taking it all in. Also, they have to be a very clear communicator who can articulate the plan in way in which every person in the organization can understand." (Mr. M. – Conglomerate)

465.   "What you need to understand is what you don't know. The whole search for me is to try to understand where things are going. You need people engaged in the broader economies – adjacent moves,

looking around corners, try to see what is happening next, talking to customers' customers, get a sense of opportunities. The hardest thing to appreciate is opportunities: 'How do I create something to meet customers' needs?' That is the hardest thing to do. Identifying the needs that make it possible. Satisfying needs. You constantly need to talk to customers. This is what corporations do not do well. Customers don't know where they are going." (Mr. O. – Chemicals)

466. "You have to realize that it not about being theoretical. It's about being practical. It's about how you can make the most of your time and effort saving money or doing things better, and inculcate that into you so that the product you are offering to the market is you. Get away from the theory. Some of best theories didn't work as in the case of Motorola, Budweiser and GM. They were once big and successful, but they are not today. Mindset plays a big role. The guys in Detroit, their ego was so big you couldn't tell them anything." (Mr. B. – Financial Services)

468. "To have the best chance for success, emphasize planning first and keep the strategic plan as full of simplicity and common sense as you can make it. If the plan is not clear and understandable with common sense characteristics, it will fail because the vast majority will not understand it and will lose interest." (Mr. F. – Financial Services)

477. "Being a CEO – leading in business – is more about thinking strategically than it is about planning. You need to form and reform your strategy faster than others with whom you compete. The most important thing is to identify the capabilities – primarily human

capabilities – necessary to pursue your strategy and make sure those are put in place. You have to build those capabilities, and then you hope that you built the right capabilities for a future that you can't actually foresee. If it takes 100 PowerPoint slides to describe your strategy, throw it away. Or said another way, if you can't carry it around in your head, it's pretty much worthless. The only way a strategy becomes real is when you make decisions on a day-to-day basis that are consistent with it." (Mr. R. – Entertainment & Media)

481. "Each year there are more and more books written about strategy, but companies still struggle with it. There is a reason your firm exists in the markets you participate in, and you need to understand your own value proposition. You need to know what is it that makes customers want to buy your product over your competitors'. Obviously – or perhaps not so – there has to be something unique about your product or company that attracts customers to buying your product. Everybody has competition; you need to understand this holistically from the customers' perspective. The first sign that your business is becoming irrelevant is when you are constantly cutting prices to stay relevant. If the firm stays on this course you end up in oblivion. You should always be seeking out or working on new ways to add value for customers so that you can maintain your margin and relevancy. This is something you should work on every day." (Mr. O. – Conglomerate)

488. "You need to watch your competition closely and try to capitalize on their mistakes. Learning from

other people's mistakes has definitely helped us." (Mr. P. – Financial Services)

655.   "Nothing ever goes according to plan. Never look at a plan and think that you have it all figured out." (Ms. D. – Consumer Products)

TEAMS

Before you begin your work together, first invest extensively in socializing so as to build genuine relationships of respect and trust. Then you can establish mutual values, shared priorities, and goals that all buy into. Having that respect and trust, having these norms in common too, will then facilitate your ability to engage in positive and constructive debate over how to perform your work best. Honor each other; honor this process. Then teamwork meets its potential – synergies greater than individuals pulling in their own ways.

3.   "Surround yourself with the right people in order to succeed. You must be able to bounce ideas off of your team and rely on them to not just agree with every decision that is made." (Mr. W. – Financial Services)

12.   "It's important to have a team environment, but not to the point that identity is lost." (Mr. T. – Construction)

18.   "Surround yourself with people that can make you successful. It would be very difficult, even for a very intelligent and hardworking individual, to succeed without a team that works well together." (Mr. A. – Financial Services)

52.   "Management always is a team effort. To think that one person can come in and be solely responsible for everything that goes on is a false perception. The

idea is to pull individuals together into a team concept. So commit to being a team person from the word go." (Mr. D. – Healthcare)

63.   "I caution you against forming a team of so-called 'rock stars.' At times it would be better to assemble less talented individuals that are able to work well together." (Mr. G. – Transportation)

69.   "I also must underscore the importance of surrounding oneself with the smartest and brightest people. By inserting people with the appropriate knowledge and ability into the right positions, the CEO can avoid being a micromanager and can therefore concentrate on other tasks more strategic in nature." (Mr. D. – Financial Services)

89.   "There is no substitute for surrounding yourself with great people. The people make the organization successful, not the systems, products, or industry. And to paraphrase Harry Truman, it is amazing how much can be accomplished when you don't care who gets the credit." (Mr. D. – Financial Services)

122.   "Get the best minds that you can around you. If you play lone-ranger, you may hit home-runs, but they will be few and far between." (Mr. W. – Healthcare)

199.   "You're only as good as the people you surround yourself with. Regardless of how great a leader, motivator and manager you are, if the people that work directly for you are less than adequate, your performance and outcome will be less than adequate. There must be an equal level of respect for and from

your employees to maintain this atmosphere. In general, you need to be fair and consistent, and if you are careful in the way you treat, reward, and praise employees, you will get people around you that respect you and that will make you more successful." (Mr. C. – Retailing)

284. "I always say when you are in the room, look at who you are meeting with and the more representation around that room the better off you will be." (Mr. R. – Manufacturing)

316. "To me, one of the most important things you've got to do is realize that it takes other people, and the success of other people, to make things happen. You can't do it yourself. You've got to have enough confidence in yourself that you want your team members – let's just say someone who reports to you – to get all kinds of praise. You can't fear that. You can't fear 'If it looks like this is all my subordinate's doing, then it is going to make me look bad; they're going to think they don't need me.' You have legitimately got to want your team members to be successful and get recognized for it. Because if they do, you're automatically going to get where you want to be." (Mr. B. – Healthcare)

323. "I think strategic management is building a team of good employees you can rely on. It is kind of cliché to say it's all about your employees, but it really is. A strategic manager must place their employees in positions where they will succeed in the future; it's a huge part. In order for a company to be successful it must build itself upon great employees and managers. They must do this by shaping the culture to fulfill both

employees' and managers' needs. I feel a positive corporate culture can create a company to overcome many obstacles." (Mr. J. – Construction)

331. "The most important thing is being able to bring people together to form a consensus that everyone agrees on. And this does not mean just the top management team, but even those on the bottom line, the person that actually gets the task accomplished. There must be a strong common bond in order for the company to be the most successful it can be. So all along the way you must consistently reintroduce, reinforce, and rejuvenate that idea." (Mr. R. – Business Services)

339. "Understand the importance of interpersonal relationships. Understand that you cannot do it alone, that you have to have people who are willing to work with you." (Ms. H. – Financial Services)

343. "When it comes to management there is a team behind senior management. The senior team must work together by understanding and appreciating how their cooperation allows the company to prosper. So make connections and build relationships so that you can rise to be a part of this imperative cooperation that takes place." (Mr. M. – Healthcare)

364. "The most important thing that contributes to your success as a manager is the people that you surround yourself with. Without a top management team that you can rely on, you cannot be successful even with the best of ideas. So never be afraid to allow others to contribute to your success. You can accomplish whatever you want, and go as far as you

want, with others by your side." (Mr. O. –
Conglomerate)

366. "I know there are a lot of people as individuals
who are great strategic thinkers and managers. But
probably the greatest advice I can give is to involve
other people. Different viewpoints and different ways
of thinking will significantly increase the quality of the
insight you bring in and the diversity of thinking. The
benefit is that often times the people that you bring in
are the people you most need to ask." (Mr. V. –
Consumer Products)

433. "Show your team that you appreciate their
expertise, and you want to benefit from it. Practice
giving credit and taking accountability. These are skills
for building a strong, trusting, high-performing team.
They are abilities you will never outgrow." (Ms. T. –
Consumer Products)

467. "I think it's really important to know that if you
want to lead an organization, you need to inspire your
people. There's a lot of leaders that do all of the
administration – all of the paperwork – but the
inspiration – inspiring people to do a better job, to
better themselves, and to work as a team – is harder
than it sounds. You really need to work on that. You
need to make sure that you can build up the team.
That's so important." (Mr. S. – Energy, Mining &
Materials)

482. "Always surround yourself with good people –
people you can trust, people that have integrity. If you
get the right people around you, it makes your job so
much easier. It's not always people like you, with the

same personality; if everybody here was like me, then we wouldn't have a great company. You need diversity – diverse ideas, diverse talents. I think diversity is real important in an organization to make the team and the chain stronger. Diverse means you've stretched and pulled; it makes the company stronger." (Mr. E. – Manufacturing)

485. "The orchestra leader can't play every instrument. The better the team, the easier the CEO role is because you can let them go on their own. This also means letting go of your ego. We sometimes forget that business leaders are subject to the same psychological challenges as everyone else, but you have to let that go and not be scared to surround yourself with the best and brightest. The biggest problem is in the human realm. Managers have egos and get jealous, but you have to put that aside to be a good leader." (Ms. G. – Manufacturing)

486. "The way to lose credibility quickly is to walk into a place and two days after you are there you say, 'I've read this book, and if you do this it will be fixed.' It's one thing for a smart-nosed MBA to come in and say that I can fix this problem and here is what we should do. It's another thing to get people to do it. The way you get people to do it is you make them part of the solution. There is nothing better than standing in front of a team and saying, 'I talked to Joe, John, Jack, and Jim, and asked them what was wrong with our process here, and they all had good ideas and they all gave me excellent input, and I think if we do this, that, and the other thing, things will be better.' That gets you Joe, John, Jack, and Jim on your side because

it is their solution too." (Mr. L. – Information Technology)

499. "The importance of relationships between co-workers is one of the hardest things for people to realize. Those are the types of relationships that you have to make work whether you like it or not. You have to mold with others' personalities the best that you can." (Mr. D. – Consumer Services)

500. "More times than not, teams matter more than individuals and their agendas." (Mr. H. – Entertainment & Media)

528. "If you can successfully train others to be able to take your job, then you are a success. I always had the attitude that I wanted people to want me to be successful, because they wanted me to help them do the same. You know, it's just so nice to know that there are people who want me to be successful. It puts extra pressure on me because I in turn want them to be equally successful in what they do. And if that happens, then we've got it made!" (Mr. C. – Financial Services)

VISION AND BIG PICTURE

You haven't come this far to be a small thinker. The world has so much to be interested in. Our world is a realm of vast and varied opportunities. Isn't there texture and richness everywhere? And it all is connected! So although the educational system is mainly rigged to focus you on detail and minutia, relax that grip and expand your horizons. Balance out the risks of narrow-mindedness, inflexibility, and insensitivity described in the introduction to the chapter on Focus. It's all within your reach.

34.   "I can't emphasize enough the importance of sharing one's vision and goals with employees. However, this sharing is not to be done for touchy-feely purposes of inspiration or motivation; it is simply to ensure that the goals and incentives – in other words, the bottom line – are harmonious between leadership and the employees." (Mr. W. – Real Estate)

42.   "You must learn to ask the why question. Don't be afraid to ask any questions no matter how big or small. It is always the question that was never asked that holds the answer to sustained growth and success. Be the one that sees the big picture and obvious details, but also be the one that brings a value-added insight. Be disciplined yet visionary." (Mr. W. – Consumer Services)

90.   "The skill and insight that is critical to succeeding in strategic management is having a vision

for the future of the firm. It is essential." (Mr. V. – Manufacturing)

120.   "The most important thing is the importance of clearly communicating your vision for the business and your strategic decisions for the future to everyone. You must know and understand the goals you want to accomplish, and look at the bigger picture to figure out how to go about accomplishing these goals. You must be able to explain to people what you are and where to want to be. It is extremely important to create an environment that can foster and promote this vision." (Mr. B. – Manufacturing)

135.   "Keep in mind that most businesses fail not due to a lack of vision but to a lack of execution." (Dr. H. – Business Services)

164.   "Leadership must have a vision for the company. The most important thing about the vision is that it doesn't change. Vision should consider even a ten- or twenty-year time frame. The strategy to support that vision doesn't change very frequently either. My recommendation is to know your vision, pick a strategy that supports the vision, and stick with it. Often, not enough time is spent at first to make sure the vision is the right vision. Along with that, not enough time and effort are spent deciding what you really want to accomplish. Once the correct vision is set, leadership must invest the time needed to get congruence with their fellow workers so that they all think that it is the right strategy and right vision. Everyone must be on the same page. Mainly, you must understand that changing the strategic vision every five years is not very stable. You can change tactics or

strategies but you don't want to change the vision." (Mr. S. – Food & Agriculture)

166. "Strive for the ability and willingness to think big. You should always be striving to take your company to the pinnacle of its potential." (Mr. T. – Manufacturing)

196. "Consider all the angles. Do not have tunnel vision with regard to any aspect of the company, whether it be performance measurement, relationships with competitors, partnerships with other companies, or even your own ideas. All things need to be considered from as many angles as possible." (Mr. M. – Healthcare)

198. "Relax! Don't go too far too fast until you know where you are. Do not get sucked into the business immediately. Take a step back, see the entire picture, and then go to work. It is important to ask big questions and see the big picture before you try to do anything." (Mr. M. – Healthcare)

223. "Students need to take the time to understand the past to be able to see the future and to stay current." (Mr. H. – Hospitality)

232. "You have to be able to correlate what you learn with looking into the future and try to predict what that future will be. You have to look at ten years down the road and think about which organizations will be around and which will survive all of this turmoil that we are seeing now." (Mr. S. – Healthcare)

309. "I would advise you to broaden your skill set and increase your overall awareness. Do the best you can by striving to understand all people. Whatever job you're in, look 360 degrees around yourself, and try to understand all of the challenges of each person around you." (Mr. R. – Manufacturing)

312. "Be very observant and study the last 10 years because you have got to see it all. You have got to see a new world of media and communications and technology. You have got to see a world crippled by terrorism which created uncertainty, which created poor economies. People got used to that environment, but it has continued for more than a decade. You saw true global images, literally a single world as it relates to communication. You saw an immense rise and an immense fall. You saw all the bad and all the good in a 10 year period, and that's informative. So study it. See what you can learn from it." (Mr. V. – Consumer Products)

320. "I think it is important that you have a long-term perspective. Don't just think day-to-day." (Mr. G. – Manufacturing)

324. "Try to always be knowledgeable about certain trends in the industry of your own particular interest. Always find out about your company's strategic plan. Understand what it is that they are trying to do, who they are trying to sell themselves to, and then find it in yourself to meet those objectives." (Mr. S. – Financial Services)

327. "If you come in and you just stay focused on your narrow niche, you're not going to have broad

experience. For example, if you come into an accounting operation, you can sit there and you can do your accounting function all day, but you should want to understand what events around the company are causing what ultimately winds up in a transaction. Reach beyond your domain and learn. Be hungry. All of a sudden you will find yourself with an endless amount of knowledge. So that's what I say: be present, learn, work hard, pay attention, and understand what's going on around you and why." (Mr. H. – Hospitality)

341.   "There are some people by nature who are detail oriented, and there are some people who by nature are big-picture oriented and actually don't like the details. They have to force themselves to get into the details. The detail person would have to force themselves to come out of there and look at the world beyond the details. So, you have to learn who you are, how you see the world, and what you really need to work on so that you don't get pegged into one role or path. If your traits are leading you down a path that says you are going to hit a glass ceiling someday – that 'I am going to hit a point where this is as far as I am going to go because my path says that I am a detail oriented person,' and you don't want to be that – you need to work on ways to expand the big picture side of your personality." (Mr. D. – Retailing)

344.   "You have to have a vision. Anyone can get lucky and start a business and make money off of it for a little while. But if you don't know where you want to go or how to get there, your luck will shortly run out. Allow me to quote Lewis Carroll, 'Any road will get you there if you don't know where you are going.'

If you don't know what you really want out of an experience or your business and how to get there, then someone will come along behind you and do it the correct way and make more money and take over your business. The other CEO will run business the way you should have been running it. Now, with a strong vision you also have to run your business efficiently. If you don't successfully use your company's resources in a manner that is cost efficient, that will also allow your competitors have a higher competitive advantage and erode your company's market share." (Mr. C. – Food & Agriculture)

363.   "One has to have vision and a set of goals. The organization needs to understand where and what they want to be in the future. They need to make sure everyone around it understands how to contribute to getting the company there. They need to make sure they have the tools to make that happen." (Mr. L. – Utilities)

364.   "As a CEO it is up to you to define a vision for the company. You communicate that vision to your top management who is then tasked to bring clarity to that vision and to make it become a reality." (Mr. O. – Conglomerate)

368.   "I don't know how to express this... You have to be able to have a vision to see where this can go and where to start. You can't just get there overnight. You have to build it by making use of your people." (Mr. D. – Retailing)

372.   "As the business environment is becoming ever more complex, more turbulent, more global and more

competitive, thinking strategically about how a firm should position itself in order to compete successfully is becoming critical. Those firms that will survive, grow, and create value are firms with a clear vision of what their competitive advantages are and how to maintain and enhance them." (Mr. H. – Healthcare)

374. "In business you can get caught up with the task at hand and lose focus on what is important. You should take time each day to step back from the hustle of the day, take a deep breath and re-focus your thoughts. This is when you will be able to see the big picture of what your day should look like and how your company should be run." (Mr. G. – Business Services)

409. "Stay educated about current events and how they affect you." (Mr. D. – Transportation)

415. "Strategic management is complex and requires insight from a lot of areas and people. You have to be dedicated to understanding the industry you want to operate in, and have a sound plan for the operation of your business. So be proactive and willing to learn as much as possible from others in your field, as well as from other fields, so you will get a more whole experience and be diversified. That way you will have the ability to piece things together when you get into a position of leadership." (Mr. T. – Information Technology)

423. "People need to see the vision, the whole picture. When you can bring it to life, they will line up to be a part of it. People will follow a leader with a

vision, so be willing to share that." (Mr. H. – Consumer Services)

425. "The main thing to remember is alignment of strategy with your mission. Managers use tactics to accomplish the strategy; but if you get lost, look back at your mission." (Mr. S. – Hospitality)

429. "A CEO's main task is to create a long-term vision for the company. Yet the only way a CEO's vision can be successful is if he surrounds himself with bright people who possess integrity." (Mr. R. – Construction)

430. "Companies that are going to succeed are always looking to the horizon and thinking about the next two or three years. Without knowing where you're going, you're never going to get there. Companies that don't have a vision for the future probably will not see much of the future." (Mr. R. – Consumer Products)

442. "Don't have blinders on. Be focused on the task at hand and do it to the best of your ability, but pay attention. 'What else is going on? Where does my job fit into this company? What is the company's ultimate goal, and how do I fit into that?' It's all about understanding the environment that you are in. Too often people don't ever look further than what's right in front of them." (Mr. C. – Entertainment & Media)

462. "Having a big picture view is tough because one of your biggest threats is not knowing what you don't know. How do you know what it is you don't know? I look back over time and get quite terrified

about what I didn't know. When I think back to when I was eighteen, the stuff I didn't know but was oblivious to – I mean, I didn't know that I didn't know." (Mr. B. – Consumer Products)

487. "The most important idea about strategic management that future leaders need to know is that strategic management should result in a vision which has been designed to be easily communicated, understandable and believable, and continuously communicated. The better it is understood by employees, the more likely they will be committed to the vision, and the more likely you will be to achieve your strategic goals." (Mr. C. – Manufacturing)

541. "Stay the course. Learn what your boss' vision is and make it your own. Never take or accept shortcuts." (Mr. K. – Healthcare)

652. "Management is a visionary field. An individual must be able to foresee opportunities, identify possible problems before they occur, and identify the good within others." (Mr. A. – Manufacturing)

WORK ETHIC

Early in my career as a banker, I was told by a respected leader, Phil Carbone, to hire good people by first looking for a strong work ethic. He showed me that virtually any deficiency can be compensated for by someone who is eager to work hard at it. So although these chapters are placed alphabetically, it is significant that this is the final chapter – the summation, the final word. You know enough. Just get to work. Some may say, "Don't work harder; work smarter." But you cannot work smarter until you first work harder – harder than others, and harder than you have before.

4.   "Work hard and be diligent. Many times luck plays a large role in strategic management, but I have never seen anyone who does not work hard run into a great deal of luck. I believe that you create luck for yourself by working hard and putting yourself in a position to be lucky. There is no substitute for hard work." (Mr. L. – Healthcare)

13.   "Being successful and reaching the position of CEO will not be given or handed to anyone. Those people fortunate or unfortunate enough to be the CEO of a company worked extremely hard to get there. The guts, persistence, sacrifice, and determination of these people is matched by few." (Mr. G. – Construction)

82.   "I have seen a lot of people with a lot of potential. However, one thing too many of them lack

is a strong work ethic. Management is your work ethic."
(Mr. D. – Financial Services)

122. "Do your homework. There is no one that ever does a good job at strategic management without doing their homework. There is information available, whether it is marketing information, consumer research, or the latest technology. The resources are endless, and there is always homework to be done to understand the environment and the nature of your product or service." (Mr. W. – Healthcare)

155. "In life there is no silver bullet. Work ethic is hugely important. Successful managers are those who are willing to put the work in." (Mr. V. – Entertainment & Media)

171. "Have fun at what you do. Often people get too wrapped up in their jobs and their lives can potentially be ruined because of it. You only live life once, and most of it is spent working, so why not enjoy your job? You might not become the next Bill Gates, but at least you will have fun along the way. A key aspect of this is to work in a sociable environment. Events outside the workplace like monthly happy hours, a softball team, or a basketball league are all signs of this. You should want to make friends with some of your co-workers. All these factors will make your job feel less of a daily burden you have to fulfill. They call it 'work' for a reason, but no one ever said it was against the rules to have fun while doing it." (Mr. C. – Entertainment & Media)

172. "Be friendly and have a sense of humor. No matter how serious work can get, you need to have a

sense of humor in order to maintain your loyal network of business and personal friends. Do not get this confused with eliminating the serious aspect of work, but being fun to be around positively affects the work environment." (Mr. Z. – Energy, Mining & Materials)

223. "Be willing to pay the pay price. You need to realize that you don't reach the top overnight. You have to be willing to pay the price to get where you want to be. You need to make sure that you get yourself out there." (Mr. H. – Hospitality)

229. "Work hard. There's nothing more gratifying than reaping the rewards that most often come as a result of hard work. That's job satisfaction." (Mr. T. – Consumer Products)

246. "You've got to work extremely hard. You've got to want it more than anybody else. I worked my way up through this industry. I washed dishes; I bused tables; I was a waiter; I was an assistant manager. I can remember counting wet $1 bills as the sun was coming up because the bar closed at 4:00 in the morning, and I was 20 years old and all my buddies were out partying. I gave all that up because I wanted to build my career and move forward. You give a lot up. You've got to sacrifice a lot. Some people don't want to do it, and that's cool. You can make a good living, be very happy, do Monday through Friday eight to five, and not have to work on the weekend. But if you truly want it, you've got to work hard, and you've got to mean it. You've got to out-fight everyone around you, because it's a competition. Especially early in your career, everybody in that same level is a competitor

with you, and that's how you need to view them. Whether you go out and have a beer with them after work, they're still your competitors. You still have to show up earlier; you still have to have a better attitude; you still have to out-work them. Any presentations that you give have to be better. You've just got to know that that's your competition, and you've got to beat them all the way around, and then you go up to the next rung. It's the same thing, the same game. The higher you go up, the harder it gets, and the more you have to work. I still work seven days a week; I get e-mails every single day. I will check e-mails on Thanksgiving and Christmas just because I want to know what sales were from the night before. So, you've got to work extremely hard." (Mr. H. – Hospitality)

250. "You must work extremely hard, do whatever it takes to succeed, have a positive attitude, and you must continually progress and change." (Ms. S. – Food & Agriculture)

251. "I would recommend over-performing your employer's expectations. Of course they will be high initially, otherwise they will not give you the job. However, in that case working hard really pays off. If you manage to over-perform the initial expectations, you will stand out of the crowd of new employees and this will give you a good opportunity for career growth in the future. Just as companies compete for customers, students who just finished their degrees compete for places to work. Of course a university diploma is an advantage, but many people have that today. What employers are really looking for are hard

working people who are committed to what they are doing." (Mr. S. – Energy, Mining & Materials)

255. "Be the first one into work and the last one to leave while maintaining good work habits. You also need to ask questions, have a willingness to learn, and volunteer for special projects even if that means more hours and no more pay." (Mr. H. – Construction)

268. "Most importantly, if you come into work every day ten minutes early, work hard, and be honest, and leave work ten minutes late, then you are ahead of the 80% of people in this world who have no work ethic at all. If you feel that you are not being rewarded based on the time and effort you have put into a company, do not be afraid to ask for more responsibility. If you are an outstanding worker, eventually your manager will recognize you. Trust me, when you are recognized you will shoot off like a rocket in that organization." (Mr. J. – Manufacturing)

293. "I am a banker seven days a week." (Mr. G. – Financial Services)

294. "New graduates, regardless of their educational background and experience, should not feel a sense of entitlement when entering the workforce or continuing their career post-graduation. Hard work is the only thing that gets you ahead in business, and the only thing that can create the opportunities that you desire." (Mr. M. – Manufacturing)

296. "Obviously you are very bright, so what is it going to take to be successful? You've got to have a

work ethic which says that if I do get an opportunity, I'm going to do this job better, faster – whatever – the best that it's ever been done and still do it right. If you can improve things, to me that's the definition of productivity. So you have to have a work ethic." (Mr. H. – Financial Services)

297. "With today's generation, people like me have a question mark about your generation's work ethic. Make sure you can convince people you have a good work ethic without just saying you have one. Point to your past experiences as an example. Then look for new challenges." (Mr. R. – Hospitality)

305. "It's important to work hard. We hire a lot of college graduates, a lot more than we used to. Banks aren't the highest paying place in town, and entry level jobs are pretty mundane. We try to communicate to those young men and women who come work for us that being a teller, that's not really exciting, but you've got to be the best teller you can be. Your supervisor has to say 'That guy or girl is great,' and you'll get noticed and move up. You've got to work hard." (Mr. B. – Financial Services)

317. "Work harder and longer than everyone else, and keep your eye on the prize. Continue to believe it!" (Mr. P. – Consumer Services)

324. "Do your job to the best of your ability. If you're trying to get noticed, never do the bare minimum. Always go above and beyond. One of the things my friend Richardson likes to ask when hiring young people is, 'Do they have 20 years of experience, or do they have one year of experience twenty times?'

Essentially, do you have a person who does the bare minimum, shows up on time, and then leaves exactly when their shift ends every day, never giving anything more than what's expected? They may be competent in what they do, but there isn't anything great about it. The 20 years of experience is someone who changes and grows with their job and their surroundings. They go a little bit further every day by doing a little more than what's asked. They often do things before being asked. CEOs often ask themselves, 'Is this employee adding any value to our organization?' If they do, those are the valuable ones. Those are the ones you want to keep around. Those are the ones you want to reward a little bit better. You try to keep their loyalty. Those early in their careers aren't going to have twenty years of experience, but they do have the ability to show the attributes associated with twenty years of working." (Mr. S. – Financial Services)

330. "When you begin your career, the first thing you must do is prove that you are willing to work hard. Your co-workers, boss, and clients will all respect you and you will be able to earn their trust. If you work hard, there will be great things ahead for you." (Mr. S. – Healthcare)

334. "I am a big believer in people working hard to be the best that they can be and demonstrating their ability to execute at that level every day over an extended period of time. I want people on my team that demonstrate they want to be the absolute best that they can be." (Mr. S. – Information Technology)

354. "Most CEOs were at least one time in their lives workaholics." (Mr. M. – Hospitality)

373.   "It's easier and more rewarding to do things the right way through hard work rather than cutting corners." (Mr. M. – Financial Services)

401.   "Today, I am finding that when I have problems with people, it is usually not because they don't have the requisite skill sets to do the job that they were employed for. It is usually because they want to play on the computer too much – they try to surf the internet. They create a conflict of interest, and show a lack of ethical competencies. It is generally not because of the core competencies that they have been trained for. It is more attitudes and behavioral based." (Mr. M. – Energy, Mining & Materials)

408.   "Work ethic is important. We had a training program at this bank, and said, 'We need a path for college graduates to come in here and go through a six-month, twelve-month training program where we can really create a lot of interaction and create the next great bankers. We gave them tons of attention; we had them going to evening functions, etc. And I was involved in trying to handpick a group of five great folks who were going to start in this program. So we picked these five folks. After six months, four of the five had quit. You don't know someone's work ethic and whether they've got it until they work here, no matter how they sound." (Mr. T. – Financial Services)

432.   "People who work hard will get pushed up the ladder very quickly. Work hard and get recognized and you can even get past people who have been there for 40 years." (Mr. W. – Financial Services)

442. "What you have to be careful about is falling in the trap of doing the least that you have to do at work so you can have the most time to go have fun afterwards. That's a good way to stay right where you started. Be eager and do the stuff no one else wants to do. Just because you have a college degree doesn't make you better; you must be willing to do the roll-up-your-sleeves stuff. So let me tell you a story about our own corporate attorney here. He truly put in the time. He would stay late at his law firm and work weekends, and the guy that ran his department at the law firm would walk down the hall when his plate was full and pass out work to the younger guys. So if you weren't there, you didn't get the work. If you didn't stay late or work weekends when this guy was there working hard – like our guy, leading by example – you missed out. Jim, our corporate attorney, stayed late at the law firm, and got a lot of that work which just happened to deal mostly with our company. So we ended up hiring him as our in-house legal counsel. He did the actual work. He asked for more work, got the extra work which led to greater experience and credibility, and eventually led him to the top. Again, it's all about showing your eagerness to learn, and there's no better way than by busting your ass doing the work no one else wants to do." (Mr. C. – Entertainment & Media)

443. "I was not well educated when I got into the business, and my kids were well educated. But the common thread was that in our 20's we worked harder than everyone else – not always smarter, but harder – so that would be my advice. Don't let anyone beat you at how many hours or how much effort you put in day after day." (Mr. R. – Transportation)

449.   "There is no easy road to success. On TV it looks glamorous and easy; there seem to be a lot of people that seem to have had success handed to them. While I'm sure there are a few that had it put on a silver platter for them, for every one of them there are 5,000 successful people that had to work very hard to get what they have. If you do something you love, it is not that painful to put a lot of time in at your work because you love doing it anyway. However, make no mistake, in order to be successful you have to be willing to put in the time and the effort. And you are going to have to make sacrifices along the way – some that you may not want to make – if you want to reach the top of your chosen field."   (Mr. M. – Consumer Services)

453.   "For many college graduates a degree gives them a false sense of entitlement to an easy salary. But what will surprise many of your peers is that employers are more interested in a solid work ethic and an established level of performance.   (Mr. A. – Manufacturing)

472.   "I think the thing that people want to see from a person with an MBA is a general expectation that the book knowledge is there, but I think people want to see a sense of urgency, passion for the right reasons is there – not self-serving, narcissistic reasons – but a desire to really help the organization, be a part of something great, and a sense of urgency to do that. People want to see that, but it's not always there. I was talking to somebody that went out and recruited MBAs for a medical equipment company. They were getting Ivy Leaguers, and they were falling on their face because they came in and wanted to be chairman of

the board in their first year. They were more motivated toward that end than they were toward results. Then the firm started working with MBAs out of state schools, and getting the cream of the crop out of there. The results were so much better; those MBAs were phenomenal compared to the others. The results were transforming when they started doing that because they were getting the top of the class – people that wanted to get out and make a difference, and didn't have the expectation that it was going to be handed to them." (Mr. S. – Healthcare)

484.   "As you look toward your future, find your passion, understand what you want to do, work at it very hard because it is tough, and then you will be successful. Start where you feel good at the end of the day and work hard. It's not easy. Nothing is, so you must work hard to stay ahead and you will be successful. You will own it. Hard work and love go hand-in-hand. The end result is that you have to find a passion and commit to it. Find the passion; go for it, and work hard!" (Mr. H. – Healthcare)

494.   "You've got to be honest, have a strong work ethic, and not be afraid to not be an 8:00 to 5:00 person. You need to be available for whatever the job requires – to find it somewhere in you to be loyal and dedicated to that company you work for." (Mr. G. – Construction)

496.   "Don't be scared of hard work serving others. Most importantly, have fun! Give back to others, serve others, and pay it forward. There is no better feeling than helping someone else out. Every little bit counts.

Being good to others is the best advice I can give, and have fun." (Mr. B. – Healthcare)

505.   "Once you get that job there is no substitute for hard work. It is important to go above and beyond and to learn as much as you can about the industry." (Ms. L. – Consumer Products)

515.   "Do not give in to the stereotypical norms for your generation; display a strong work ethic, be patient and do not require rapid gratification of your needs. And pay close attention to details." (Mr. S. – Manufacturing)

517.   "If you did not put in all of the hard work that you do, you would never achieve success. The same goes for every job you have. You can't look at it just as a 9:00 to 5:00 workload. The job will have to be carried on into the rest of the hours of the day also. Some of the best ideas I get come from when I am not at work. To be a successful CEO it has to be a life, not a job. People will see the work that you put in on the job, but the true success comes from the hard work you do during the off-time. I think that is what people will benefit from the most." (Mr. H. – Utilities)

518.   "Outsmart and outwork the people around you. The secret to success is not waiting around for someone to do it for you. You're in charge of your success and your destiny. If you're not getting the help that you need, reach out to someone and ask for help. Don't wait until you're unmotivated." (Ms. K. – Consumer Services)

Work Ethic

519. "Work overtime. Ask for more work. Don't be afraid to take on more work than you think you can handle." (Mr. F. – Manufacturing)

526. "Everyone looks for an employee with a good work ethic and who is passionate about his job. No doubt, that is the most important thing I can share with you." (Ms. M. – Business Services)

533. "Nothing comes easy. You will have to put in more than just a 40 hour work week to achieve your goals." (Mr. R. – Consumer Products)

556. "Work hard. In this day and age hard work has been replaced in some aspects. You will find it beneficial and fulfilling to put effort into what you do. To see something come to fruition that you have poured your sweat, blood, and tears into is a great experience. I think all young people entering the workforce should understand that things take time. Only people who win the lottery become wealthy overnight, and I don't like those odds." (Mr. N. – Energy, Mining & Materials)

epi-logos

Irony: Seeking advice, then not implementing it.

What you do matters far more than what you know.

The words that you are least comfortable with hold the most potential for you to learn and grow.

Don't bother spending much time on the words that you agree with.

Now that you've been through this, what are you going to do differently?

Pass it forward. Become a mentor. Share the gifts you've been given. That's the point.

Stay in touch...

ABOUT THE AUTHOR

Gordon F. Holbein, Ph.D. is a Senior Lecturer in Strategy & Leadership at the Gatton College of Business and Economics at the University of Kentucky. He was born and raised near Syracuse, NY, and went to school in New Hampshire, New York and Pennsylvania, but much prefers Kentucky's milder climate!

Gordon's education includes a Bachelor of Arts in Geography from Dartmouth College, an M.B.A. from Syracuse University, and a Ph.D. in Strategy and Leadership from The Pennsylvania State University.

He has twelve years of work experience in bank management in New York, predominantly in branch management, product management and strategic planning. His consulting experience extends across organizations in the automotive, healthcare, financial services and technology industries, and he has worked with a variety of not-for-profit organizations as well.

Dr. Holbein's academic career spans more than twenty-five years of university teaching at UK, Penn State, Syracuse University, and Northern Kentucky University. His main areas of expertise are Strategic Management, Leadership Development, Corporate Social Responsibility, and Global Management.

Professor Holbein left the ranks of the University of Kentucky's research faculty in order to pursue a full-time teaching career in 2000, and was promoted to Senior Lecturer in 2007. He teaches in UK's undergraduate, graduate and executive education programs.

Dr. Holbein has been recognized by the University of Kentucky's College of Education as a "Teacher Who Made A Difference" on three occasions, has been cited for excellence in teaching by Beta Gamma Sigma Honor Society, Alpha Kappa Psi professional business fraternity and the UK Panhellenic Council, and in 2012 was named UK's best professor in the Kentucky Kernel's "Best Of UK" awards. He has also been awarded the Humana Corporation Teaching Innovation Grant three times.

Gordon has been a featured speaker for the Emerging Leader Institute, the University of Kentucky Student Activities Board's "Final Word" symposium, and in the Delta Epsilon Iota Honor Society's guest lecturer series.

Made in the USA
Lexington, KY
02 September 2016